Trans-Africa by Motorbike

A father's diary

by

Lawrence Bransby

Cover Design by CLIVE THOMPSON - cliveleet@mweb.co.za

Please note: I have published this book without photographs to lower the purchase price. As we live in the digital world, I encourage you to go to www.hareti.co.uk, my son's website, where you will be able to see a large selection of photographs taken during the journey described here. (The e-book, however, has been published with photographs.)

INTRODUCTION

When I was twelve, my father, elder brother and I walked from Umhlanga Rocks, just north of Durban, to what was then Lourenco Marques in Mozambique, a distance of some 375 miles.

The adventure emerged from the many long walks the three of us undertook together on Sunday afternoons through the sugar plantations and virgin coastal bush which covered the north coast of Natal in those days, following overgrown paths smelling of wet mould, with grey wood moths the colour of shadows and the sounds of unseen birds and snake-lilies like small fires in the undergrowth; of balancing on the winding rails of the sugar cane train which puffed its way busily along rustling contours, tooting with urgent high-pitched squeals whenever it came across us in the way.

Those were good days, being twelve amongst the rolling green of sugar cane, with clod fights and bows and arrows and a bonfire in the back-yard which my brother and I tended for eight uninterrupted days during a school holiday, creeping out in the early dawn to coax it into flame with titbits of twig; a time before the tyranny of girls...

And then, on a blustery day deep inside the rustling green of the cane, it was decided: we'll do a long walk; an *adventurous* walk.

I don't remember who suggested it first, but it emerged and was seized upon with that excitement which constricts the chest and makes being alive in this mysterious world wonderful.

My mother was compliant, the maps dusted off. I can remember tracing the road with my finger where the orange of South Africa changed to Swaziland's brown and then the exciting foreign pinkness of Mozambique, with names like *Inhambame* and *Inhica* and *Inharriem* and little spiky tufts which the legend assured me were swamps. And it was then that the compelling and addictive bug of adventure travel sank its fangs deep within my psyche so that now, at a much more advanced age, its sweet venom courses just as strongly through my veins as it did then.

What twelve-year-old could forget walking through the silent dusty streets of Chaka's Kraal in the frost-pale darkness of early morning, water-container icy against fingers covered by dragged-down jersey sleeves... a crashed train, mangled and torn, around a corner of some obscure rail line between grassy hills somewhere in Swaziland... a blustery night on the sawdust floor of a railway goods wagon where we had stolen to escape threatening rain, the clank and bang of a loose door mingling with the moan of wind and the lighter, more precise taps of rain; and being terrified during the night that the train would clank and begin to move, taking us somewhere into the dark night... coming across the bloated stiff body of a cow in the road, the stench of blood and dung hanging heavy in the cold morning air... the clang of a police cell door where we had requested shelter and the stale smell of urine and despair that hung about the place, laying our home-made sleeping bags on the cold floor, a high, barred window set deep in whitewashed walls... a sweet-cold orange flung by a black man driving a refrigerated truck in the shimmering heat of midday, the road straight and endless and slow... hunting for firewood in the dark and under-cooked dehydrated peas crunching between the teeth... cold spaghetti eaten from the tin with a shared spoon and a rustling delicate mouse in the torchlight nibbling Marie biscuit crumbs from a discarded packet, so tame and unthreatened that we could stroke it?

The images are personal and precious, small oases in my consciousness as fresh now as they were decades ago.

Two years later, we rode by bicycle to what was then Beira, a distance of 1200 miles, using those wonderful old black, single-speed, rear-wheel-pedal brake, Phillips bikes we had in those days. We scorned the three-speed bikes available at the time (only weaklings need gears and we were tough - although I coveted those gears in secret and wished we could afford them) and we rode our iron steeds more beloved than girls, hardy as tractors and unbreakable.

I can't remember when this second trip was decided, but I believe it was again on one of those blustery walks across green rustling fields of sugar cane, the rail tracks being ripped up in favour of Mercedes trucks and progress, the quaint era of the chuffing trains gone for ever. Walking was too slow, we declared. Bicycles - that was the ticket!

And so another bike was purchased second-hand for my father and off we went with, I believe, the reluctant blessing of my mother. We met the great Red Adair in the bush of Mozambique putting out an oil fire. (He spoke American like an actor in a cheap film and my brother and I laughed out loud until we realised he wasn't acting). We drank dark red wine from tin mugs and stale rolls with Portuguese truck drivers, unshaven and bogged to their axles in mud somewhere along a narrow track in the bush far from anywhere. "When it's gone, it's gone!" they shrugged philosophically when my father asked whether they had enough for themselves. Then into tsetse-fly country, trying to ride through soft sand with the dreaded flies biting our arms and back and neck, falling off in the dust when slapping at them. I remember weeping silently where my father couldn't see me and wanting it all to end. Then my father on hands and knees, kissing the tar when the dirt road ended, faintly ridiculous but we laughed our relief that the worst was over... cooldrinks at roadside stalls and a mouldy bun, hard like a cricket ball, from a Portuguese trader woken from his corrugated iron shack in the bush early on a Sunday morning. In a town, talk of the bodies of shot Frelimo piled in the bush, dowsed with petrol and burned...

I can remember crouching on guard in front of a crackling fire, deep in the Gorongoso wilderness, squeeze-bottle of ammonia (our naive weapon, carried strapped to the cross-bar of the bikes) in my terrified hands, listening for lions. A four-hour stint, frightened of things in the shadows beyond the firelight as time dragged its feet, the sleeping forms of father and brother increasing my isolation; and then, next morning, a hundred metres along the track, the heavy pug marks of a lion...

The memories are there still and they are mine. No one can ever take them away or the modest achievement of our journeys. And I believe I am a better person now because of them. They gave me something I still carry with me now.

When my wife and I married, our first vehicle was a Land Rover and we honeymooned across the Kalahari desert, the Okavango swamps and Moremi and Chobi game reserves - special times in Africa's wildness. And then, over the years, Namibia and the mountains of Lesotho and Botswana again and again, seeing the wilderness areas so desperately loved diminishing as tar roads and tourists and fences and civilization paced across the land with relentless efficiency. We always regarded ourselves as travellers, never tourists, and the joy of pulling off the track and into the elephant-smashed bush or camping next to a mountain stream unsullied by the filth of previous campers was something to be cherished. Before our two children were born, we yearned to cross Africa in our Land Rover, but sadly we belonged to a pariah nation and the taint of our white skins and South African citizenship blocked us anywhere north of Rhodesia and Malawi. At one stage we toyed with the idea of forged passports but then Gareth came along.

Our children - Jemma was born two years after Gareth - joined in with our lifestyle as children do. I can remember Gareth tipping himself, strapped in his bouncy-chair, head first into a river in Lesotho at the age of 7 months; and Jemma's car-chair hooked over the back seat of the Land Rover, bouncing her to sleep as we negotiated mountain passes.

Gareth always had to have his own fire in Botswana, apart from ours, which he would tend lovingly; and both children learned to drive at a young age along sandy tracks, far from other vehicles or people, gaining confidence. I remember watching a 15-year old Gareth doing doughnuts in the Land Cruiser on the Magadigadi Salt Pans where he thought I couldn't see, and a twelve-year-old Jemma driving off by herself into the shimmering distance, raised on a pillow so she could see through the windscreen.

And then Jemma got her first horse, taking after her mother, and Gareth an off-road motor-bike like his dad.

He and I rode together in the vast plantations around Ixopo where we lived for thirteen years, and in the mountains of Lesotho, following bridle paths up mountain valleys and alongside snow-fed streams, no fences and no people save an occasional blanketed Basotho herd boy with his sheep and Angora goats.

Gareth never raced, was never interested in competition, but he developed over the years into a competent rider who grew to know his and his bike's limitations; and he grew to love the wilderness. Together we rode to the top of Thaba Ntlenyana, Southern Africa's highest mountain. He was twelve at the time, I think. I'm sure he is the youngest person to have conquered the mountain on a motor bike and from then on we did it each year. (I'm sure he's one of the youngest, at seventeen, to ride a motorbike across Africa, but who knows? We weren't out to set any records.)

When Gareth finished primary school, 12 years old, he and I did our first long trip together - across Lesotho; heavy rains turned the "roads" into muddy tracks but, although the XR200 that he was riding, with its load of camping stuff and extra fuel, was far too big and heavy for him, he coped well and we had a great adventure.

But land without fences and where animals roam freely past one's tent is becoming less and less available, and the threat of human predators in the bush and on the streets far outweighs the danger of attack by lion or elephant or buffalo. And so, despite the initial euphoria after the release of Nelson Mandela and the rejoicing over the New South Africa, things in the country began to slide. Armed robbery became an ever-present threat; gun-shots heard at night elicited little more than a raised eyebrow. Our house was burgled regularly, despite our large dogs; farmers developed radio networks, erected electric fences and added to their armouries. Then one night the daughter of a friend was shot in the back while opening the gate to their farm, a friend was shot through the chest when he surprised robbers at a trading store, a man was sprayed in the back with AK47 bullets when he overtook a Combi Taxi too closely. We had to instruct Jemma, while riding her horse alone in the plantations, to keep an eye open for people and, if she saw anyone, to immediately turn and run. And then we had to ban her from riding in the plantations at all.

Sadly, we felt it was time to leave South Africa. Our children had set their hearts on university education and South African degrees were being regarded with suspicion internationally. We decided, after much soul-searching, discussion and prayer, to emigrate to Wales. Glynis and I resigned our jobs. This was July; we would fly to Wales for Christmas, sort out the immigration technicalities from inside the country, and not come back. (A decision, incidentally, with unseen repercussions for Gareth and me on our trip later.) It turned out that I needed to return to South Africa after Christmas to sort out various things and it was then, in August, shortly after our decision to emigrate, that, in a moment of glorious anticipation, I made my decision: I would ride back to Wales by motorcycle. I could fulfil the dream of a lifetime.

Quite by chance, at 45 years old and with a family to support, I was temporarily unemployed, had time, money and a logical excuse to do the trip that would have been impossible at any other time. I put it to Glynis and, bless her, she accepted. (Rather bitter, I am sure, as my mother must have been when left behind on our Lourenco Marques and Beira trips, but she never once expressed it. I am indebted to her for that and for - dare I say it? - allowing me to go.) And then the thought: why not take Gareth with me? He had just turned seventeen and had his learner's licence; the Welsh school term only started in September - he would effectively miss a year of school, but what's a year when you are young?

I put it to him and he accepted. No wild excitement, but that is not his way. Just, Yes, he wanted to come. No, losing a year of school didn't matter...

Was I trying to rewrite history, do with my son what my father did with me? If so, it wasn't a conscious decision. It wasn't planned. The trip just happened on me, and what can be better than sharing such a dream with your child? We had five months to prepare. The pundits recommend a year. That, as well as preparing for emigration, made it a busy time.

Most important: the bikes. Both Gareth and I had 200cc trail bikes, two-stroke things of great speed and acceleration, but not suited to the long haul. I also had two 1970 BMW 50/5's that I had picked up as a job lot, the one still in pieces, and considered long and hard as to whether to do the trip on them. It was an enticing challenge but, in the end, we rejected the idea as impractical. In retrospect, it was the right decision. They are road bikes, old, formidably heavy and, although reliable, not made for laden rough-road travel. We opted for Yamaha XT500's, 1981 models which we bought cheaply and which are renowned for their robustness and simplicity of design. In fact, they were, in spirit, the black Phillips bicycles my father, brother and I rode to Mozambique, heavy, slow, unkillable. They have points and coil ignition, easy to repair along the side of the road, easy to find spares for. The engine has about 5 moving parts, the gearbox said to be so over-engineered it could be used to drive a tractor.

We couldn't afford expensive aluminium panniers so I made one from galvanised sheeting. We constructed carriers from angle iron for the jerry cans, water bottles and the thousand and one other things necessary for the trip. When our full set of tools, spares, clothes and rain gear, tent, cooking utensils, stove and basic food, sleeping bags, camping mattresses, two Jerry cans and three water bottles were all laid out on the floor of the spare room just prior to our departure, despite having pared our load to what we thought was a minimum, it seemed impossible that it would all fit on the bikes. When Glynis saw it she laughed. We made up tank bags out of old army hold-alls which hung off the petrol tanks bringing some weight forward; sleeping bags and camping mattresses were attached to racks bolted on in front of the handlebars and above the headlight. The rest was strapped onto the angle-iron frame we made to fit behind the rider, but which had to clear the swing-arm and allow space to kick-start the engine - no electric starters on these bikes.

We tested the loaded bikes only twice, once on a ride around the house to see whether a six-litre water bottle could be carried on the handle-bar carrier (it couldn't - all the bike wanted to do was lie down), and a short trip into the plantations, fully laden. On this trial, the bike was manageable, but up a steep path, the front wheel wanted to lift with only small acceleration because of the load behind the rider.

With time running out we could test no more. It was time to fly to Wales. After Christmas Gareth and I would return to South Africa and, rushing to beat the sun to the Sahara, would set off within days of landing.

AUTHOR'S NOTE:

I have published this diary - except for this opening introductory chapter - almost exactly as it was written on the trip (except for some basic editing). I purposely have not attempted to turn it into a travel book, and have left in all the little personal touches, thoughts, emotions and frustrations, just as they were written at the weary end of each day. This, I feel, gives the writing and the trip a realism which captures far better the actual day by day incidents without the filter of retrospect, just as it happened. I hope you will gain a better feel for the trip as a result and, even more important, I sincerely hope that, after reading it, some of you will decide that embarking on a similar trip - hopefully taking one of your children along as I did - is not as difficult as it might seem and that the rewards vastly outweigh the hassles.

WEEK 1

Day 1: Tuesday 14 January 1997

I didn't need the alarm to wake me. From outside came the sound of cows demanding to be milked, but I wasn't asleep. Gareth was. Nothing keeps him from his sleep.

I woke him. "Today's the day!" I said, excited but afraid too.

We dressed in silence, wrapped in our own thoughts, and then, sitting on my bed in our riding gear, we prayed together.

The bikes were already partially loaded; we completed final packing and mounted them before the sun rose. Both started first kick (which I took as a propitious sign).

After a week of rain the day was beautiful - an endless blue sky overhead, weak early morning sun and fluffy semi-transparent clouds like looking at thin ice from under water. The bikes sounded healthy although, as usual at the start of a long journey, I listened with heart in my throat to every change in engine note like a parent at the bedside of an ailing child.

The dirt road after the turn off from Himeville was good, damp from the rain but firm, and the XT's rode as if they had been designed for just this - dirt roads, the blue mountains of Lesotho looming out of the clouds ahead. Riding the bikes as loaded as they were, however, was not going to be easy. I was only too well aware of our lack of thorough testing. On the rough, the bikes, particularly mine, proved to have a disconcerting propensity to want to lie down. Fully laden, we would be carrying about 90-100kgs plus ourselves and, although we have spread the load as far forward and as low as possible, the back wheel still carries the lion's share.

Now usually an off road bike, so long as the front wheel is held steady and straight, will tackle almost any terrain with enthusiasm. The back wheel can flap and bounce about, try to overtake the front wheel, whatever, but so long as the front wheel is straight and has grip, the rear usually knuckles down and follows obediently after. Not the loaded XT's, though. The slightest degree off vertical and, instead of slipping sweetly back into place, the load merely tries to fling the bike onto its side and pitch the rider - me - along with it. Most disconcerting. I have to watch the bike like a hawk.

Unfortunately for me, a few kilometres along the dirt, well before the Lesotho border, we hit a stretch of that smooth, wet, yellow clay that motor-cyclists dread. Immediately my front wheel slipped out; I tried to counter but all that did was fling the load over the other way and after another and more exaggerated slide I was off. My left leg, caught under one of the Jerry cans, was wrenched quite badly and the knee immediately started to swell. Gareth was ahead of me and disappeared around a corner. I managed to extricate my leg and desperately tried to get the bike up before the backup party - who were following to bid us farewell at the top of Black Mountain Pass - arrived, but the damn thing was too heavy for me to pick up. The madly photographing group arrived, much to my humiliation, to see the bike ignominiously on its side, Jerry cans scattered across the road and me attempting to walk as if I wasn't hurt. Then Gareth appeared from around the corner having missed me behind him and destroyed the last of my tattered dignity by having to kick-start my bike which had decided to sulk.

Disconcertingly, Gareth claimed that his bike wasn't slipping: was it the tyres - he had Michelins and I had the cheaper Kenda - or was it an indication that I was losing my touch, that age was catching up with me at last? Was I kidding myself that, at 45, I could do this trip? Furthermore, disturbing noises had been coming from my bike on the way to Sani Pass, accompanied by jerks and hesitations; I just *knew* it was a slipping clutch and wondered whether it would be possible to make it up the pass without anyone noticing. There was no way I was going to abort the start and head back to Pietermaritzburg to have it repaired. The *ignominy* of it. The shame. I would soldier on blithely and get the repair done quietly further on where no one would know us.

At the border Gareth told me loudly, "Your chain's slipping - didn't you hear it?" which put the final nail in the coffin of my dignity. I left him to tighten it while I sorted out border formalities. He has his uses. The pass itself was tricky but not impossible. Whilst riding up, the nostalgia within me was strong; so many wonderful holidays had started from there; so many memories. And this might be the last time we will see it.

We rode on through mist, winding our way along the rutted track up and over the Drakensberg Mountains and into the Kingdom of Lesotho. By now the sun was up, the sky so deep blue it was almost purple and just sufficient chill in the air to keep me fresh. Final farewells at the top of Black Mountain Pass where we looked out at the hazy ranges of the Drakensberg Mountains disappearing into the distance and then we were on our way, Gareth and me, alone.

The continent of Africa ahead seemed very big indeed.

Suddenly I was struck by a dreadful pang of loneliness. In Wales over Christmas we had been with family; in Creighton over the last few days we had stayed with friends and now, suddenly, I was alone. Yes, I had Gareth with me, but my aloneness was caused by something else. It was the lack of a home with a wife, the familiar comfortable surroundings, the predictability of it all, that I felt so heavily. I missed Glynis and our home so badly it was like an ache. (Isn't it sad that the realisation of the importance of a relationship strikes one so strongly when one is apart and, when together, things are so much taken for granted?) The Lesotho roads were beautiful -

smooth dirt and well maintained; so different from our travels across here many years ago. I remember in the early days having to dig the Land Rover out of a large water-filled pothole it had slipped into, wedging itself against the bank; standing on the bumper while Glynis drove to help with traction; driving at walking-pace over tracks that looked more like the rocky beds of rivers.

We stopped at Mokotlong for petrol, parked our bikes alongside tethered Basotho ponies and donkeys loaded as only donkeys can be loaded throughout the world. A small crowd of blanket-swathed Basothos stood about in silence, watching. Then on, riding a little faster into the afternoon as our confidence grew, but conscious of the deceptively smooth roads covered in places with a loose layer of gravel on which the tyres slip like riding on marbles.

We lunched next to a river, crystal clear and so fresh that afterwards we stripped off our clothes and bathed, watched with interest by the occasional passing herd boy or man on his pony, going somewhere within the purple anonymity of the mountains that surrounded us. The river was cold, all about us the sound of running water, green young wheat, smells of cow dung and damp weeds, toadstool huts, mountains and more mountains. Truly God's own country. The valleys are warm but on the ridges a cold wind buffets us as it always does in Lesotho.

As each familiar spot passed, rich in memories - a camp site here and a lunch spot there; there we had to wait for a flooded river to subside and here we were washed out by the rain - again my thoughts turned to Glynis who shared all these special moments with me and the children over the years, and I was sad and lonely.

My bum, back and knee were aching by the time we reached the Katse Dam turn-off. The dam, when completed, will fill these stark valleys with a blue ribbon of water and change forever the precious remoteness deep in these mountains. We stopped briefly to look over the already filling valley then rode on into the setting sun before finally leaving the road and setting up camp on an exposed and blustery ridge high up in the mountains. The sun quickly faded behind dark clouds and the air turned unpleasantly cold.

We have travelled 325km and are tired. Despite the bath in the river, our bodies and clothes are dirty and covered with dust. Tent up, sleeping bags laid out, I boil water for tea while Gareth takes off his tank to look for the cause of an annoying oil leak which seems to be coming from his steering head bearings. Oil has also been forced into the glass cover of his temperature gauge and the waterproof covers of our sleeping bags have rubbed through in places. All this after just one day. Sitting alone in the calm shelter inside the tent with my cup of black tea, Gareth tinkering with his bike outside, again there comes upon me a feeling of such profound loneliness that it wrenches at my gut.

I want to go home.

Now. Straight away.

When camping in the bush or on the open plains of the Magadigadi, this was always our special time. Glyn would make tea and we would sit and savour it while the aches died away and the air cooled towards evening. Then, clean and fresh smelling from a bath in the bucket, we would sit in front of the fire and have our traditional sherry in the bottom of a mug, and the peace of the evening and the companionship of each other would fall upon us.

Here, now, I am dirty and sore and alone. And Africa is such a very big and frightening place. Why, I could be sitting at home now in front of the TV, warm and comfortable and secure. 320km and 1 day. Only another 19,680km and about 4 months to go...

The reality and the dream are always so different. Why aren't I just an ordinary conventional person who *reads* about adventures instead of doing them?

Supper of two-minute noodles and tuna cooked by Gareth, black tea and in bed with a book to read by candle light. Not really so bad after all, but still lonely in the pit of my stomach and more than a little scared...

Day 2

I woke at 5:30am after a good night's sleep. Rested until 6:00am, thinking about the day ahead, worrying about the trip as a whole, and then made tea. Outside was a calm Lesotho dawn, with the cries of herd boys and the clonking sheep bells across the mountain slopes only serving to emphasise the stillness. Smoke from distant cooking fires rose straight up and the sky was a clear pale blue.

We tried to make breakfast with an obstinate and sulky stove. Can't complain, though, the instructions said *don't* use leaded fuel which, of course, we were using. I hacked thick slices off a slab of home-cured bacon - a going-away present from our friends - and par-cooked them then made the foolish mistake of adding two very runny eggs to the pan. After about 15 minutes and still a milky mush in the bottom of a luke-warm pan, I started packing up while Gareth worked on the stove. When finally it was 'ready' I could only eat a mouthful before feeling very sick. I couldn't swallow the salty mush in my mouth and spat it out behind the tent, trying to keep my fear from Gareth. (He told me later that he too was feeling sick. My sickness is worry about the enormity of the trip; Gareth thinks he is getting flu.)

But, as always, once packed and bumping along the cattle path which led to the road, my spirits soared and I praised God for the beauty of his creation and the wonder of being alive. Riding motor bikes in the wilderness does that to one.

Part of my lifted spirits is, without doubt, the fact that we have (after looking at the Michelin maps of Africa in the tent last night) decided to change our route, leaving out Botswana and Namibia and heading straight for Zimbabwe. The road I had hoped to travel in Botswana was one Glynis and I drove on our honeymoon - a wilderness of a road, two sandy tracks through the Kalahari for about 400km. But on studying the map I see that it is now a tar road so most of the adventure of it has gone; and, although Namibia is a wonderful country to tour, the distances are vast long straight flat tar roads, hundreds of kilometres long. But the most compelling reason is that, were we to take that route, we would in a way be going backwards to go forwards and really I need to make even the *semblance* of progress to the north. What if something were to happen and the trip had to be aborted before we have even got out of South Africa? The embarrassment! At least get beyond the Tropic of Capricorn and, even better, the Equator so that if the unthinkable happens we will be seen to have made some ground.

Then, also, the threatening spectre of the Saharan heat - what will it be like? How will the bikes cope? Will we, loaded as we are, be able to ride over soft sand? Up to Kenya should be the easy bit; thereafter a daunting unknown.)

We reached the Katse Dam wall by 8:00am and paused to take a photo showing the rapidly filling dam; a young Basotho horseman on his beautiful pony presented himself in front of the lens with a wide smile and a formal pose - just the perfect touch to make a special photo.

Then on, following a newly-built tar road which snaked up and down steep mountain passes - a biker's delight - hard right, foot scraping the road just a touch, then hard left then back right, the bikes happy and not trying to lie down all the time (or else we are getting used to the unfamiliar weight). Then finally through the border, the South African side already degenerating into third-world world sloth and filthy ablutions.

We stopped at Bethlehem for lunch; neither of us hungry but we ate from a sense of duty. Whilst sitting at our cafe table, dirty and tired, Gareth asked me how far to go to Heidleberg where we hoped to camp. I added up: just over 200km. I saw his face fall and he admitted to feeling rather sick. And again, the enormity of what I have undertaken came over me: day two and Gareth is ill. What will I do if he becomes seriously ill far from help, somewhere in central Africa, in the desert, perhaps? What will *he* do if I become sick? Is it wise to take a seventeen-year-old on such a demanding journey?

The responsibility hangs heavy on my shoulders.

What would I do if I lost him, if he died? How could I tell Glynis?

We decided to go on a little further to Frankfort where we are now camped next to a river, the tent pitched on newly-mown grass under the shade of a willow tree. Tea is made and a few clothes washed and we both feel better.

After a lie down, Gareth and I went over the bikes. Although the engines sound healthy, there have been a few little problems over the past two days: loose engine side cover stud, loose chain, oil leaks. My speedo stopped working today and with it the milometer. Fortunately Gareth has been his usual reliable self, happy to whip out the tools and attack the problem. So far all have been sorted out, but I do hope these teething problems stop soon - I wouldn't like to have to sort out two "problems" a day for 90-odd days.

A glorious evening: Cape Turtle doves 'how's fathering', hadida's screaming at the setting sun, the still water of the dam in front of us and tinned savoury mince and veg for supper. During the night, as we read in the stillness of crickets, an owl hooted above us. Wrapped in our sleeping bags, we paused to listen in the flickering half light of candles...

Day 3

Supposedly a cake-walk day, the 200km to Half Way House began with a flat rear tyre on Gareth's bike, discovered as we set off fully packed and laden from the camp site. How can a brand new Michelin tyre fitted with a new, double-thickness enduro tube be punctured after only two days' riding? If this is going to happen on tar, how will we cope when the roads get really bad?

We hand-pumped the tyre and rode to the local dealer we found just around the corner, unpacked, wedged a Jerry can under the engine and removed chain then back wheel which we handed to the experts; a thin piece of wire had penetrated the tyre and tube. After a two-hour delay we were off again to suffer the traumas of negotiating the freeway through Johannesburg. (Gareth's first drive on a freeway - illegal on his learner's license - and he had to do it on a loaded XT. Traumatic stuff but after an overshoot and a quick U-turn across the flow of traffic and through a small gap in the central reserve under a bridge(!) we reached Half Way House at about 12.30 where we are staying with friends.

I am very concerned about Gareth. He is not well - he has a sore throat which I am trying to treat, and the sun has penetrated a small gap between his helmet and goggles and has burned the tip of his nose. Although I am older, I think I am more resilient and I don't want to push him too hard. I keep trying to get home to him that he must tell me how he is feeling and if he needs a break. But Gareth, at the best of times, says very little. The burden of the trip has given me a bad headache; the going is so painfully slow and the distance so great. 920km so far.

Day 4

I woke in the early hours to the sound of thunder and a flickering against the curtains. A strange sound was coming from outside - rain. Heavy rain. It had a depressingly set-in sound. After breakfast it was still pouring down so Gareth and I donned our bright yellow plastic cover-alls. We looked rather silly - like a combination between spacemen and Arctic sailors. The electrics on Gareth's bike are playing up; they only work when the bike is running. Another worry.

On the freeway to Pretoria we were snug and dry, the very cheap all-weather suits working well. A bakkie slowed next to us and a young man leaned out the window. "Where you from?" he shouted.

"Ixopo," I called, wishing I could have said Wales.

We seem such frauds all kitted up and looking the part - spare tyres, Jerry cans, water containers strapped to the bikes - like city tourists on safari wearing camouflage gear and leopard-skin hat bands, but really we are only a good day's straight drive from home in a car.

"Where you heading?" he shouted.

"England -"

"Good luck!" he called after us.

Later, in Pretoria, another car drove alongside us and a young man put his head out the window, waved to attract our attention and then called out, "Good luck!"

Strange how good that made me feel. Why should they wish us luck? Perhaps they were earnest young men yearning for adventure themselves and saw in us kindred spirits, their called good wishes an attempt to link their psyches with ours.

We found the British Consulate easily. I left Gareth with the bikes and walked in. Inside it was cool and impersonal. My riding boots clacked over the smooth tiled floor. I asked for the Entry Control Officer, expecting/hoping to be told, "This way, sir, he'll just be a moment -" and then a cosy chat, perhaps a cup of tea, stamp in the passports and away. Permission to enter the UK granted. New life begins...

Instead I was given a ticket No. 36 and motioned towards a door. Large bare room; many bored-looking people; rows of seats. Number on the wall machine said 13. I took a seat. Waited. Looked around. Set my stop watch. Yawned. At four minutes, still 13. Went outside to get Gareth. That took about ten minutes; back to the room. Still 13...

Said Hi to the young man sitting next to me and observed jokingly that we might as well go and have coffee somewhere. He replied, using many adjectives beginning with 'F', that I could order and consume a Big Mac and chips and *still* have time. He had No. 16 and had been sitting since 8:00am. It was now 9.30am. Quick calculation (the wall machine *still* said No. 13) and Gareth and I, after a brief whispered conversation, decided to take our chances at Dover. We had given up 15 minutes to political correctness and now we were heading *north!* The die is cast.

Filled up with petrol and Gareth noticed that his rear brake lever adjusting nut had stripped. What next? His bike seems to be falling apart by the hour and we are only in Pretoria. Bought two nuts from the garage, quick cup of coffee and back on the road.

The weather was overcast but dry and glorious to ride in. We were soon out of the suburbs and heading along a straight road across yellow grassland dotted with acacia trees. The bikes purred. My spirits rose. Signs to Warmbad and Nylstroom and Potgietersrus flashed past. They brought back such good memories of previous journeys to Botswana. I wished Glyn and Jem could be here to share them.

And so we rode all day, from 8:00am in the morning, with stops about every hour and a half for this and that, until 5:00pm. Everything was glorious. The bikes put their ears back, shrugged off minor ailments and said cheerily, "We can do this all day!" and they did. 2:30pm and Pietersburg - half way to Zimbabwe from Pretoria where we were going to stay and we said, "We're feeling strong! Let's do another quick 100km and sleep tonight at Louis Trichardt. We can be at the border by 9:00pm!" and off we went, bits between our teeth.

We paused at the plaque marking the Tropic of Capricorn for a photo and were saddened that so many idiots, desperate for some tenuous immortality, had felt the need to spray their names on the natural cluster of boulders which surround it.

It rained in spells throughout the day and, as each downpour started, we would pull off the road, whip on our plastic yellows and be off again. We could see the heavy showers ahead and watched the bright ribbon of road dodge between them, great dark clouds dragging a pale gauze of rain behind them as they swept across the land. A strong side wind was blowing, buffeting the bikes about. Trucks, too, tried to brush us off the road, treating us with contempt. They will pass leaving about a metre space and then, before clearing the bikes with their trailers, gradually pull in. On your left, the edge of the road, sometimes a nasty drop which can have a bike over in a jiffy or rip a tyre; on the right, thundering wheels, chest high and half an arm's length away. Needless to say, the trucks always win.

Passing trucks are interesting in another way: as they get within about two metres of you, first there is a brief and disconcerting suck back followed by a tremendous blast which pushes you violently away. This is immediately followed by a strange period of calm as one enters the bubble of air travelling along with the truck. The bike immediately accelerates because there is no head wind, as if it is trying to race. A quick tap off, reducing speed, allowing the truck to get ahead. Then the back wheels rush past; a brief hiatus, still caught in the bubble of dead air and then, suddenly, mad shuddering buffets of wind, left, right, top, pummelling you and the bike as nature struggles to fill the vacuum. During this time you try not to fall off, lose the road or get caught beneath the passing wheels. Keeps one awake.

We swapped bikes for an hour or so today and noticed interesting little idiosyncrasies: Gareth's bike seems to rev 1000rpm slower (unless the rev-counter is out), runs eight degrees cooler and covers about 60km per tank less than mine. Its engine rattles and clanks a little - probably loose timing chain and worn cam shaft, but nothing too serious, we hope. She's very willing. My bike, all told, is tighter, smoother and, in terms of mileage, much younger, although they are both 1981 models. Still, time will tell...

Then, as the afternoon waned, the road narrowed, more potholes appeared, a dead goat lay in the roadside gravel and pinpricks of rain touched my cheeks. Ahead, dark clouds massed over the hills of Louis Trichardt. There is a feeling, at last, that we are on our way.

Later and it is dark. Gareth cooks supper in the light of a candle while rain taps urgently, in sharp little pocks, on the nylon of the tent overhead. Inside, it is comfortable and cosy...

Day 5

It rained all night and we woke damp and even wet in places. There are small leaks in the tent which we will need to look for and seal. Gareth's throat is still sore.

We were off by seven into thick mist and rain. After a few kilometres, we stopped to take the hiking mattresses off the front carriers because they obscure the lights and I discovered that my headlight doesn't work. Gareth rode in front, barely visible through the mist, over the mountain range under which Louis Trichardt nestles and down the other side into patches of blue.

At the Zimbabwe border we were descended upon by four "facilitators" offering their services. These are young men who buy the official forms (handed out free to us) from the officials and "facilitate" your passing through customs and immigration for a small fee. A kind of acceptable bribery, if you like. I chose one to facilitate and appointed his friend to guard the bikes. He quoted R50 at which I burst into hysterical laughter, patted him on the back and told him what a good joker he was. He said to pay him anything I wanted.

Then followed the whirlwind. He quickly removed from us our passports, bike papers and whatnot, and filled in all the forms for us in an indecipherable scrawl. He declared, in writing (without asking us anything), that we had nothing of value to declare to customs, no cameras, radios or alcohol and only "personal clothing". I pointed out to him that, actually, we had a camera and a radio. "No problem!" he assured me, passing the unchanged form to be signed. And no problem it was. I paid him R20 and he asked me for a little more to bribe the policeman. I gave him another R2.50. Back in the car park our guard was on duty, attempting to look efficient. No problems. Whispered conversation between the two. Our 'guard' then informed me that our 'facilitator' had complained to him that we had not paid him well, that we were, in fact, stingy swines.

"What!" I cried, anguished. "I paid him R20 for 20 minutes' work!"

At which our facilitator looked sheepish and smiled. The two had done a deal to split the proceeds and he had told his friend, the guard, that I had only paid him R10. So much for honour among thieves. (We left them while they were engaged in a somewhat heated discussion.)

We were into Zimbabwe. A blustery day, heavily overcast, wind ruffling the long grass like cats' fur. Bulawayo 330km. It was a lonely road, but not unfriendly. The cool weather and the long green grass and the straight road were welcoming somehow. A flat land, covered with green scrub bush veld, goats and baboons - wily creatures both. They pause on the side of the road, look left, look right, look left again before crossing. But no people, no shops, no farmhouses. In 100km we saw one man walking along a fence, three women sitting next to a stream and a boy on a donkey cart. Nothing. Where are all the people?

By mid-afternoon the weather turned ugly. Throughout the day, rain had pricked our faces intermittently and we had worn our cheap plastic rain gear, but now it was mizzling steadily with a harsh wind blowing. Having been riding for nearly eight hours, we were tired, wet and getting cold. The thought of putting up a tent was not a happy one. I decided that we could spare the price of a hotel for the night.

The Plaza Hotel, Bulawayo, is a seedy joint where the middle aged-women who lounge on the verandah with drinks and cigarettes in their hands evoke tired images of prostitution, and the men look like bookmakers too knocked about by life to make a deal. We walked through the bar terrace to the office, managed to scrape up enough South African rands to pay the bill and toted all our stuff up to the room. I think anything left on the street would have been gone in minutes. Four beds, two rooms, deep bath with worn enamel. Shivering, we spread all the wet stuff, including tent, over the two spare beds to dry and lay down to the chorus of drunken patrons watching a soccer match below our window. On the TV we could watch a country and western singer or a country and western singer or more of the same, but at least they had three channels. Later from the balcony which overlooked the street we watched two drunken men fight on the pavement below, swinging wildly at one another while they tried not to fall down.

After dark, washed and warm, we investigated what was to be had for supper. Fish and chips. In the bar lounge we were jostled by noise and the smell of stale beer. I felt uneasy. "Hope we live through the night," I commented jokingly to Gareth. A black man from an adjoining table leaned over and introduced himself. His name was Sylvester. "You know, I'm more Rhodesian than Zimbabwean -" he said, mock conspiratorially.

His friend was Steve and we joined them. Talk was quite difficult because of the surrounding noise and accents, but they said how happy they were in Zim, how they wouldn't go to South Africa if we paid them, what with the violence. Zambia, they felt, was a backward country. Kenya, Steve said, was good, just like Zim, because the British had been there a long time too!

The breakfast menu on the wall offered:

TOASTS WITH JAM
SIGIMENTS OF FRUIT
CORNFLAKES WITH MILK

Gareth and I ate and talked in relaxed camaraderie discussing the bikes, the day gone by, our hopes and plans for Zambia and

Malawi. We plan to go slower, take side roads if possible, explore more, swim in the lake...

The waiter came with the bill and asked, "How was the taste?"

Day 6

Affter an exhausted sleep, we both woke drugged and still tired. A good breakfast and then I changed some US$ with the owner of the hotel - a short, fat, balding Greek man with an open-necked shirt.

"I've got a problem," I began.

"You've only got *one* problem?" he laughed. "I've always got problems. You lucky..."

The fairly short 280km we thought would get us to Vic Falls turned out to be 457km, so we girded our loins for another long hard day and headed out of town at a late 10:15am. Had to use the petrol carried in our jerry cans for the first time as we neared Vic Falls. The day was overcast with fine spickles of rain. But as the day progressed the cloud separated, exposing patches of blue until it was almost clear and very hot. Thousands of yellow butterflies drifted across the road and massive beetles like miniature flying armoured cars lumbered about. One hit me on the helmet while we were riding and for a moment I thought someone had lobbed a stone at me.

Interestingly, today has been the first really hot weather on the trip so far and an unpleasant reminder of what might lie ahead. The sun is still clearly to the north of us at midday and heading in the same direction as we are. I hope we will overtake it and get it behind us soon. Thoughts of the Sahara make me afraid.

The bikes ran steadily for six and a half hours. We travelled slightly faster today - about 84kph - to make the distance. It is almost as if, realising we mean business, the bikes have given up trying to thwart us with petty breakdowns and are working with us willingly. I try not to anthropomorphise them, but in a way it's hard not to; they are our close companions for most of the day and they react to our commands, have bad and good days and show signs of strain just like people do. They are still machines, but how wonderfully designed! I roughly worked out (on one long stretch of road) that by the end of the trip each piston will have travelled through the bore some twelve million times.

And Gareth tends them with loving concern. I think I'll leave all the maintenance to him. He's a natural at it, constantly checking, planning ahead and studying the manual. He's like a rock, my son is. Strangely mature and yet dreadfully naive in a sort of knowing way. He rides with the maturity of a 45-year-old, never fooling about, never clowning, never showing off. I suppose he has nothing to prove which is a good thing. In fact, to my knowledge, he has never shown off at any time which suggests someone at peace with himself. He is a good companion.

I was worried at first that there would be a tension between us but there hasn't been, not for a moment. It's always concerned me that there has been so little communication between us, as if we were drifting apart, but now I know it's not that. We both of us don't communicate much; 'taciturn' is what Glynis calls us. (I would choose 'reserved', but I am biased.)

In the many hours trapped within the bubble of one's helmet, one does a great deal of thinking. And it is good to think, to have the time to. I talk to God quite a bit, especially in the morning as we set out, ask for protection over us and Glyn and

Jem. Ask Him too to make sure Glyn is desperately lonely without me so that she will know I am special in her life. I have a fear that she will get on so well without us that she will wonder whether I am worth putting up with when we finally reach the UK.

One so desperately needs to be loved and respected by those who are close - spouse and children mainly. I think to myself what I can do to make sure it happens but, of course, there is nothing one can *do*; one just *is*. And one's spouse and children know one so intimately that any planned action or series of actions will be seen for what they are - a charade. One can act for strangers but not for family. They see you when you wake up in the morning, for Pete's sake, and when you have no clothes on. There's no hiding there.

Last night I felt a lovely bond with Gareth; in fact, there has been from the start, like fellow conspirators.

Enough of that...

We reached Vic Falls after 4:00pm. At the municipal camp site some young men surrounded us and offered carvings, black market money, dagga and told us to go to the Elephant Hills camp site out of town because it was better. (I wonder whether they pay them to do that?) We drove out and set up camp. Checked the bikes. Gareth found a bolt missing securing an oil pipe and his 'O' ring chain master link is badly worn. This is most worrying. We have come 11% of our journey along very good tar roads (except for Lesotho) and daily the bikes (mainly Gareth's) seem to be disintegrating, a little at a time. I sometimes wish we were doing the trip north to south get the bad stuff over with first and then the good. Now we will have to face bad roads and isolated and primitive conditions on bikes which are getting progressively more worn.

I was sure I had an 'O' ring link on the spare chain, but not. Damn. I have about 5 spare links, but no 'O' ring. I had meant to get some before we set off but in the final hectic rush I didn't. Gareth put the spare chain on - a rather worn one - and I will try to get a link sent to Nairobi.

As evening descended, we went to look at the water of the Zambezi flowing past. Some locals were fishing for little fish about the size of the last joint of a finger. I could understand much of what they were saying.

"What language are you speaking?" I asked.

"Ndebele," they said.

"It's a lot like Zulu."

A white man who was standing nearby turned to us and said, "Chaka drove them up here," then, *sotto voce*, he added, "But they're still all a bunch of kaffirs." He was a veteran of the Rhodesian war, wounded in the knee and working at Vic Falls. Loves the country but hates all blacks.

A young woman camping next to us told us she had been diagnosed as having malaria and had suffered terribly with it over the past ten days. She was on both types of anti malaria pills too, just as we are. An added concern. The onset, though, seems to be quite slow and fairly distinctive; if we get infected we should have about two days to get to help. I questioned her in detail about the symptoms: headache, fever and sometimes diarrhoea and vomiting.

We ate supper outside as the sky darkened, mosquito coil burning and skin covered with repellent - then we lay on the grass and looked at the sky. It was beautiful and peaceful. Then into the tent to read by candlelight. The air is very hot, and the burning candles make it worse. Outside, a mad beating of drums - more of a display for tourists, plastic and unsatisfying. It doesn't evoke in my breast that primeval fear of the dark continent, mysterious and wild, that we have come to find.

Day 7

A bad day! A bad bad BAD day!

We got into the town of Vic Falls late and I was foolishly tempted into changing money on the street. Needless to say, despite all my wisdom regarding these matters, all the warnings in "Africa on a Shoestring" I was taken for $150 and given a *huge* wad of Zim $2 bills enclosed in one Zim $20 note during a surreptitious exchange in a cafe toilet.

They are both blue, just a different shade... And the man seemed so trustworthy...

There were clear warning signs, but I ignored them all. First, he insisted on doing the transaction in a toilet. Claimed that, because the transaction was illegal, we would be arrested if we were seen by the police. Second, when I disputed the exchange rate, he agreed with me but didn't bother to make any changes to the fat roll of Zim dollars he had in his hand. And my other errors (stupidities?): not checking that *all* the notes of similar colour were twenties and not just the outside one, cunningly obscuring the rest which were all twos (I mean, how stupid and naive can you get?); and, finally, if I were the slightest bit suspicious (as I was) why didn't I just change one $50 traveller's cheque instead of three? If it had worked out, I could have returned to change more later.

Stupid! Stupid! Bloody stupid!

To give him credit, he was very convincing; the wad of Zim dollars in his hand was impressively large and his ability to vanish the moment he had poissession of my three signed travellers cheques was admirable.

To punish myself, I was not going to launch myself off the Victoria Falls bridge (attached to a bungee cord, of course), but Gareth insisted - mistake No. 2. We booked, made our way onto the bridge (refusing the offer of a taxi ride to cover the 500m to the bridge) then stood and watched a few other idiots doing it. It is, at present, the highest bungee jump in the world.

Then it was our turn.

Gareth went first, stood calmly over the 1100ft drop with his toes over the edge and launched himself into the void in a perfect swallow dive. Fifteen minutes later he was back, grinning, and shouting, *"More!"*

It's silly but understandable, I suppose, how parents like me watch their children for signs of strength and weakness. I was proud of him, chalked up a cross on the CHARACTER list in my mind, sub-heading "Bravery". I suppose children do the same where we are concerned, weigh us in their minds...

Now my turn.

I didn't want a countdown, wanted to stand on the edge, calmly think about what I was about to do, look down at the river far below, savour the moment to its full intensity and then lean forward over the edge and jump - which I did. What an amazing experience! The most frightening thing I have ever done. A chaotic, mind-numbing fear; a tumbling through space towards the great Zambizi River so far below it's like a thread... and then, as the bungee slows my fall, I begin to spin. Up and down, gracefully spinning. I come to a stop and spin... and spin. I don't know why. On the video, Gareth didn't. I do. And my notoriously weak stomach rebels.

For the rest of the day I have felt weak and bilious; I feel so still now.

We were given certificates saying: "This is to certify that XXX has momentarily lost it and thrown himself off the Victoria Falls Bridge, the highest bungee jump in the world."

Tomorrow we enter Zambia. We have been on the road for one week. It seems like a month. This afternoon we gave the bikes a good check over, cleaned the air filters, found the problem with our lights: Gareth's - fuse; mine - broken earth lead to the battery.

I am positive the bikes will rattle apart piece by piece before we reach the other side of Africa. But there is nothing we can do but keep riding and keep checking.

WEEK 2

Day 8: Tuesday 21 January 1997

It rained hard during the night. In the early morning we were awakened by the clatter of baboons and warthogs knocking over the dirt bins. We emerged from the tent to a still overcast day, packed up wet tent and equipment, and were through both borders and into Zambia by 9:00am - most friendly and helpful.

The difference between Zimbabwe and Zambia is immediately noticeable. Zimbabwe, with its tree-lined roads and cut verges, its well kept game reserves and very good roads, lacked somehow the feel of 'Africa', that wild, untamed, somewhat frightening wilderness that one looks for in this continent. Obviously this is not entirely so; Zimbabwe has its wilderness, but this was not perceptible to my senses as we passed through. It was almost civilized.

Zambia, however, is different. The word that comes immediately to mind is 'ragged'. The road signs are rusty; the grass is long and uncut on the verges, bush and scrub encroaches to the road edge, not cut back like in Zimbabwe. The houses are older, lower, as if slowly sinking back into the earth with rust from the roofs, paint and plaster flaking from the walls. It still has a colonial feel to it: single-story houses with wide fly-screened verandahs, small one-street towns of flaking pastels, men on bicycles carrying impossible-looking loads of charcoal and women walking along the roadsides carrying babies on their backs.

Wanting to look at the Railway Museum in Livingstone, we offered an old man an impressive-looking Kwacha note of fairly high denomination to guard the bikes but he waved it away with disgust. It was worthless...

As we exited Livingstone, we were met by a road block with soldiers - many of them women - clutching guns; along the road, a lone soldier patrolled every bridge. Why it is that the poorer the country, the greater the need to show military force? How will that lone soldier protect that bridge and who in heaven's name would want to blow it up anyway? All are very friendly, though.

Wanting to phone Paul and Nikki Cumming with whom we hope to stay, we tried to find a telephone or rather a telephone that worked. Because of the valuelessness of the Kwacha, K100 notes are almost worthless, so how does one stuff enough coins into a slot to pay for a call? And the copper telephone wire along vast sections of road has been stolen; it made me homesick for South Africa where stealing copper telephone wire is a national pastime.

We stopped at a farm but their phone didn't work.

Along the way Gareth spotted various old engines: Lister, Bamford and a stationery steam engine which we just *had* to inspect. Anything that has an old engine makes Gareth's eyes glitter.

The road to the farm was sandy and it was sobering to note just how badly the bikes perform in soft sand, slewing from side to side and almost impossible to keep straight and upright. Any idea of riding through miles of soft desert sand can be ruled out: they simply won't do it. (Or, more likely, we don't have the skill to make them.)

At lunch we stopped at the small town of Choma. Gareth waited with the bikes while I tried again to phone; no luck. And then, almost without warning, the heavens opened for our first tropical afternoon storm. We huddled under a rusty shop verandah and watched the rain catching the sun's rays with bright flashes, cascading from the gutterless corrugated iron roof in front of us in small waterfalls. Then, as quickly as it had started, it was over. Roofs dripped and the street gurgled like a small river. The air smelled wet and warm and colours were suddenly more bright - a wonderful feeling of equatorial Africa.

I bought two long French rolls and two oranges from a shop and we lunched sitting on the side of the road just out of town, opening a tin of sardines.

It was a long day's ride, but beautiful with the bright sun and black sky with the occasional bright splash of a sunflower poking through the tall grass. On the sides of the roads the land was sodden and huge puddles had formed. At every little town, stalls offered tyre repair and second hand tyres, and from trees hung strips of inner tube called 'leggin', used to fix or *'bhopa'* (tie down) anything from a popped bicycle tyre to a broken car spring. Whatever is broken gets *bhopa'd* with this stuff.

We reached Mazibuka at 5:15pm and I managed to make a call from an official post office phone. Nikki answered and directed us to their home - another 33km on. Finally, exhausted, we found it along a muddy farm road.

We have been made welcome in this home of virtual strangers; Paul, a mechanic, Nikki, daughter of a missionary, and their two young children. After a quick supper and bath we all went to a fellowship group they attend, and now, back home in my room (smelling sweetly of the little girl we have ousted), I am at peace. I have been worrying about our route to the Central African Republic: we have to go either through Zaire (at war) or Sudan (at war) and finally Algeria (Moslem fundamentalist war). But the topic tonight was God's provision for us through the good and the bad - a message, I thought, intended just for me. And then there was this song:

"Because He lives I can face tomorrow,
because He lives all fear is gone,
because I know He holds the future
and life is worth the living just because He lives..."

Just outside our room was Prov 3:5-6 framed: *"Trust in the Lord with all thine heart and lean not unto thine own understanding. In all thy ways acknowledge him and he shall direct thy paths."*

OK, then, I will.

Day 9

Today was spent working on the bikes with Paul. He and Gareth tested and analysed and read the wiring diagrams in the manual (I gave up because they were talking Greek, and worked as a spanner boy and messenger). They found the fault: a blown regulator so I faxed Johannesburg for a spare, as well as 'O' ring links and points to be sent to Nairobi. (We never got them.)

The new Zambian president, Frederick Chiluba, seems to be well liked and the people I spoke to feel that the country has reached a plateau. But theft is rife, AIDS has reached shocking proportions, well-intended but paternalistic Western aid mostly leaks out along the way before it reaches those who really need it - the same old story.

Why is Africa like this? The phones don't work, the hospitals are a danger to your health, the school system is chaotic, AIDS is rife, the people mostly just *survive* on subsistence farming, the officials are corrupt...

Paul commented wryly, "In Zambia, amongst the local population, it's not how well you live but the fact that you *are alive* that counts." Paul and Nikki's children attend private schools and, if anyone gets badly sick, they are flown to South

Africa for treatment. Last week Nikki's father, who runs a clinic and a mission station fully supported by himself, drove 100km during which time he came across no fewer than five government vehicles - mostly new donated Land Cruisers - which had crashed or rolled (there had been a bad rain storm) *that* day. All provided by international aid...

I will try to say no more...

Day 10

Said a very sad farewell to Paul and Nikki Cumming and their delightful 4-year-old Bethany, and made our way along the muddy farm road back to the main Lusaka highway.

At the Kafue Bridge we stopped and took out the packet of Dad's ashes (carried stuffed in a tank-bag) and which we were going to sprinkle into the river. Glynis' father, it seems, had been happy and fulfilled during his Lusaka days and it seemed fitting that we bring part of his ashes here while the remainder will be cast into the waters of the canal below the farm in Wales.

At the bridge, I looked about - no soldier or guard in sight. Took out my camera and was sighting for a shot when from a tent concealed in the under-brush to one side of the bridge burst a soldier, moving rapidly and purposefully towards us, shouting and waving his arms. I sighed inwardly, wondering whether I was going to be arrested and locked up for ever, then leaped into my fast-talking, hail-fellow-well-met, lovely day isn't it, how are you? routine, telling him in earnest tones the story of my father-in-law and Gareth's grandfather and how he had died etc etc. "Please could we just, you know, sprinkle some ashes -?"

"It is not allowed," he replied firmly and determinedly.

I was going to ask whether stones, Pooh sticks, bottles, pieces of bread were also "not allowed" or whether it was just the ashes of dead grandparents but decided it wasn't worth it. My smiling face and grovelling must have worked because he softened a little and allowed us *one* photo, but NO ashes. Ashes were still, "Not allowed".

We left quickly and wandered around small muddy roads for a while, trying to get to the river by another route but couldn't. Finally we walked into the bush on the Kafue flood plain, found a lonely looking tree and both Gareth and I sprinkled Dad's ashes onto the long grass underneath its shade. I thought for a moment of him as a younger man, pioneer of sorts, a Welshman living out his days under the African sun.

I hope, if he knows, he will be satisfied.

We had been told that the Salvation Army in Lusaka would put travellers up reasonably so we entered the sprawling and rather run-down town, found the place and after much negotiation got a rather expensive room. Then on to the Tanzanian Embassy which we found very easily. I was expecting to have to come back the next day or even wait over the weekend until Monday but, with the minimum of fuss, a polite official took US$30 off me, four photos and passports and said, "Come back at 2:30pm".

We found a bank, changed some money and waited while the heavens opened for the afternoon storm, then back to the room to read and rest. Later I left Gareth, returned for the visas, took photos of the Lusaka Hotel and the Cairo, Great North and Great East Road signs for Glynis who had lived here as a child, and then tried to find their old house at 13 Devon Close. Didn't find it then, but later Gareth and I went out again and, incredibly, we found the place. The street had been re-named but it was still a 'close', it backed onto the cemetery as Glynis had described and it was No.13. So strange thinking of my wife playing there as a little girl, all the stories she has told me over the years. I do so wish she could have been here with us. I looked especially hard just for her.

After dark we rode around some seedy looking streets, looking for food. Street vendors and vagrants shouted at us but we ignored them until we realised that we were riding down a one-way street. Quick U-turn and embarrassed smiles and waves. We found an open shop so stopped and, leaving Gareth to guard the bikes, I ran in and bought steak, onions, mushrooms, rolls, marge and Cokes. When I emerged it was very dark and both Gareth and I felt exposed and vulnerable. We quickly started up, shrugging off the sellers and the beggars and, our backs tightening with the expectation of a mugging, we sped back to our room. Later, like two conspirators huddled over the paraffin stove, we cooked a steak supper many would kill for.

On the radio while we ate, more reports of fighting in Sudan and Zaire. It seems our path north is blocked. But there is nothing we can do but press on steadily and make the final decision in Nairobi. (The radio has just announced that the military rebellion in Central African Republic has been resolved. We didn't even know there *was* one.)

Day 11

It was good to get away from Lusaka, away from the dirt and the diesel smell and the rushing cars. Everywhere we stopped, people tried, with maddening insistence, to sell us something or, at the very least, engage us in personal conversation - only, after contact has been made, to lean forward conspiratorially and ask in lowered tones for money. "Honda, Honda!" little boys shout wherever we are. (It seems that *all* bikes in Zambia, regardless of make, are Hondas.) *"Bafana Bafana!"* others exclaim when they hear we are South African, referring to the South African soccer team.

Cities are ugly places, depressing and lonely, and it was good to head out into the countryside again. The weather was grey and mizzling and we wore our yellow rain suits all day. The skies looked depressed. We bought large mushrooms from sellers on the roadside and pressed on, the road narrowing and becoming more and more potholed. It keeps one awake, though, dodging them and working out the best route through patches where the road looks like it has been hit by mortar fire.

At about 11:00am the heavens opened and the rain deluged on us, continuing to do so for the next three hours. We stopped at a roadside bar for a Coke, the radio pumping about 3000 very fuzzy decibels out of 10w speakers. That seems to be the way they do it in Africa - always a radio playing at speaker distorting volume. Men stared at us from the shelter of the verandah where they sat drinking, clearly resenting our presence; after a while one sidled up to us and asked for money. I declined his request and he sullenly shuffled off. The atmosphere became more strained so we drank our Cokes quickly, pulled our rain jackets about us and left.

The continuous rain was starting to seep through our defences; by midday we were wet and getting cold. We stopped under a small thatched "hut" for shelter and made hot soup for lunch - that and a roll, a tin of sardines and some dried fruit. Some galvanised iron containers had been placed under the eaves to collect rain water so we filled our water bottles. From now on we will have to be careful about the water we drink. So far, thank goodness, we haven't had to use water purifying tablets: four drops of tincture of iodine per litre of water. Disgusting stuff.

We pressed on in the pouring rain through hills covered with virgin bush, up and down, shrouded with mist. The land was sodden, all the rivers bulging and pushing at their banks; streams flowed across the road, inches deep and dangerous to cross. I think we are going to get a lot of this further north and will have to learn to cope with it and how to keep dry. Unfortunately we are going to hit Equatorial Africa at the height of the rainy season.

Finally, at about 3:00pm, we descended a little and the rain stopped. The sky was still grey, but lighter and more friendly. We have come 310km and it is enough. We followed a track off the road, winding steeply through the bush to the very top of a hill where a repeater station has been built, and set up camp. Everything is pretty wet, sleeping bags included. I strung up a washing line between two trees and we draped everything over the bikes and wherever we could find space; Gareth made tea and we lay down on our mats to read, the late afternoon still and hushed; all about us is the clean wildness of natural bush. In the blue distance, across ranges of mountains, lies the haze of Mozambique.

Day 12

I have just bathed in a tin bucket, the water as hot as I can take it, the soap so strong it made my eyes sting. The bathroom is a rough out-house with a hanging door, low ragged thatch roof and so scrubbed that I feel cleaner than I have for a long time.

We are in Malawi at a 'Guest House' about 20km inside the border. The owner, a small man with sad eyes, welcomed us graciously and showed us our rooms - rough, low, corrugated iron and pole roof, bed and table and chair at which I now sit and write. His thin wife heated water over a fire for our baths while a young child peered shyly at us from a safe distance just outside the door. Only the man speaks to us; his wife and children smile shyly with averted faces and go about their business, although all the time keeping contact with the corners of their eyes. The toilet, a long-drop, smells strongly of carbolic acid. Both it and the 'bathroom' were cleaned as soon as we arrived, the cement floor left gleaming wet.

After my shower and craving something sweet, the sad-eyed owner arrived at my door with a smile and an enamel plate filled with newly-picked and washed mangoes. I devoured three and then settled to write...

Back to last night: As the darkness of evening settled over the land, we retired to the tent to read by the cosy glow of a candle. Then we heard voices approaching. We tensed, afraid. Three men. They greeted us from the darkness outside the tent flap, informed us that they were guards of the repeater station. Expecting to be told to move off, I readied myself for some discreet grovelling.

"It is dangerous to sleep here," the spokesman said. "There are many thieves. You must come inside -"

We demurred, cosy and settled, not wanting to move. They were insistent. "It is dangerous. We will protect you. You must come -" They had an axe and two heavy sticks as weapons.

Thankful but reluctant, we roughly packed up our belongings, took down the tent and, with their help, carried everything into a concrete-floored room. Here, they said, we would all sleep. We laid our mattresses down and read for a while under the harsh overhead lights. Wondering whether we were keeping them up, I volunteered, "Any time you want to sleep, you can turn the light off -"

"Oh, no!" they assured us. "We sleep with the light on!"

Despite concrete floor, bright lights and damp bedding, we both slept well.

At 6:00am, however, smiling broadly, our hosts informed us that they were knocking off now. We had to leave, they insisted. Still drugged with sleep, we packed up quickly. Outside it was drizzling lightly. I was grumpy, expecting the knowing glance, the covert hint asking for payment, but none came. They even helped us carry our equipment back to the bikes and then waved us a cheery goodbye. What delightful fellows they had been and how I had misinterpreted their kindness and generosity.

We had nothing at all for breakfast, it was 6:15am and drizzling. I wondered what the day would bring, whether it would rain all day like yesterday, how long we could survive in the wet. Our persons, bedding and equipment are vulnerable to constant heavy rain and I am fearful for the future.

We set off carefully down the steep winding track through the bush to the main road. And almost immediately I felt good. There is something so special about riding a motor cycle through beautiful countryside. My tiredness fell away, the pinpricks of rain were refreshing, the cool wind in my face invigorating.

The motor cyclist, exposed as he is to the elements, feels each change of mood of the world about him. Not, obviously, to the same extent that a walker or cyclist does, but enough to make it significant. When the wind blows it jostles you; rain makes you wet (well, it does if you are poorly equipped like we are); the sun warms or burns you; you feel the temperature variations at the top and bottom of hills, in the shade of a valley or when a cloud obscures the sun. The earth breathes its smells on you as you pass: the warmth of the tar, wet earth after rain, a dead animal in the bush, smoke from an open fire; diesel too, the smell of cows and cooking food, passing through a gum plantation. It makes the world somehow three dimensional and one feels more alive.

Shortly, though, the drizzle stopped and we rode on through a cool overcast day. My bike is running exceptionally well, as if it has got its second wind and could take me, Gareth, both our loads and Gareth's bike all the way to Wales. Gareth, sadly, is troubled over his, and I wonder whether he rides with his stomach knotted in fear of a major breakdown. He doesn't complain, though. But whenever we stop he lets his engine run and crouches to listen to it clank and rattle and ping in the most disturbing fashion. It is clearly rather worn and not in the pristine condition we were assured it was when we bought it 2nd hand from Johannesburg. Anyway, except for a major overhaul, there is little we can do about it now.

While riding during the morning, I felt a distinct sense of *deja vu*. Exploring this feeling I realised that I was experiencing, just then and in the flesh, my many hours spent dreaming before the trip started. Always, before, in my mind's eye, I would see myself astride a bike with purring engine, a load at my back, the green bush of Africa passing by on either side, a narrow straight road disappearing into a distance tinged with blue, dark skies with towering clouds ahead.

And I was doing it. I was actually *doing* it.

My dream has become reality and it feels *so* good!

While the morning was still fresh and damp, we stopped at a small town whose name I cannot remember. Many of the buildings showed the clear architectural influence of Portugal and I realised that we were only 20 or so kilometres from the Mozambique border. We bought some newly-baked bread, still hot and smelling of yeast, stopped just out of town and, on the side of the road, watched by a group of children and some cows, we breakfasted on fresh bread, thick with marge and Marmite.

The countryside is beautiful, the villages and small towns picturesque. Usually the roads are clear and almost deserted, but as we approach habitation, the road ahead becomes filled with movement: goats, bullock carts, men riding bicycles, women carrying children and loads on their heads, small black pigs with rotund stomachs. The bicycle is to Africa what the *bakkie* is to South Africa. Anything and everything is carried on it: wife and child, a trussed fully-grown pig, sacks of flour, up to three crates of cool drinks all (except the wife and child, obviously) *bhopa'd* with the universal African answer to rope and the cable tie, long thin strips of inner tube. Many wave and call out as we pass and we wave back, feeling like the queen.

For lunch, mangoes, bought on the roadside, yellow and firm, all I could eat. We sat in long grass next to a muddy dam while cattle munched contentedly alongside.

During the afternoon, we came across a primitive barrier of rocks laid across the road. Having heard stories of robbers stopping cars and trucks in this way, we slowed, found a gap and hurried on, glancing behind and to either side of us into the bush as we sped away.

Then on, with 25km to the Malawian border town of Mchingi; we passed through with no problems, the border officials more interested in an Africa Cup soccer match which was being transmitted loudly over the radio - Zambia vs Malawi.

Having done our day's mileage we looked for a place to camp, but all very populated. No matter how far off the road we went, following small paths through the bush, within minutes of stopping, little brown heads would pop up, as if out of the very bush itself, and stand, watching.

Exhausted now and wondering whether we would ever find a place to set up camp, we saw the sign to a guest house and here we are, clean and comfortable.

A scrawny fowl pecks in the dust outside my door. In the distance a radio plays. The air is so still that sound carries far...

Day 13

Our host, dressed in a white shirt and tie for church, presented us with a gift of bananas before we left and wished us God speed. His wife was sweeping the hard clay courtyard clear of leaves, using a cluster of twigs as a broom.

The land is flat, the road still following the railway line, populated almost without a break with small clumps of huts, their thatch untrimmed and hanging like a too-long fringe; meticulously cultivated fields of mealies and tobacco cover the land which is clean and unlittered. Small towns with two-roomed shops and petrol stations appear regularly and, at intervals, gaily-dressed crowds disgorge from rickety churches and pour down the road. Most of the houses and huts are built with a semi-fired brick, pale orange in colour, and at every settlement one sees a kiln of fired bricks either complete or partly used. The land is dotted with mature mango trees, leaves so dark as to be almost black, set in the fields about 30m apart so that one gets the impression of riding through a scarcely populated bush veld rather than cultivated land.

Later the sky turned dark; a strong wind started to blow, buffeting the bikes. We raced a squall of black clouds threatening rain for 80km until it caught us but, although we stopped to put on our plastic suits, the rain was half hearted. It has been a mizzling kind of day. Then we entered the main street of a small town, dull buildings and people lining the street; the wind blew a flurry of dust. Suddenly all about us were swallows, darting and diving, twisting and fluttering in front of our wheels just there and nowhere else. It lifted my spirits.

Why just there? I wondered.

We by-passed Lilongwe and headed towards distant purple mountains. At the top of every rise I looked for the water of the lake. Eventually, in the early afternoon, we reached Senga Bay, a small town about two kilometres from the beach. Of course, the bay has been developed by a hotel and we have had to camp in the hotel camp site, but we have little choice. There is a rest house in the village but we need the contrast of water just metres in front of our tent.

It is sad when one looks for the wilderness places of Africa and so often find hotels offering water skiing and demonstration tribal dances. But the lake is beautiful, calm and grey, reflecting the skies; the wind has calmed and, after a lunch of mango, banana and bread, Gareth and I went for a swim, the water clear and clean and strangely warm. It is fresh too, although it looks like the sea.

Day 14

Late last evening, Gareth and I went for a walk along the rocky coastline of the lake, huge rocks piled and tumbled, small waves lapping against them and thick forest rising steeply above. A fish eagle cried plaintively and circled above us. We came across rock-rabbits sunbathing; then, attracted by their squeaks, climbed through a gap in the rocks and into a hidden cave where hundreds of bats clung to the rock ceiling and flitted through narrow passageways close past our faces. It was damp and smelt of wild and dead things. Later we sat on a rock with an old fisherman with long yellow teeth. His legs were thin, his knee caps like deformed knobs and the soles of his feet were grey and cracked. His name was Myros and all he had caught were two small fish the size of my thumb.

We asked him if he could organise a local boat to take us out to the island today and he agreed. I am so tired of being a tourist, of doing the tourist thing. The hotel has a boat, takes trips to the island, but I want this bony man with his two small fish to have our money instead, take us perhaps in his patched and rickety boat...

That, in a way, is what this trip is about - to try to experience something of the real Africa. We like to think of ourselves as travellers, not tourists, with connotations of brash, wealthy, camera-clicking people in shorts and loud shirts, the package-tour brigade where you stay in a hotel that is the same as any hotel in the world and eat the same food and sleep in air-conditioned bedrooms and see the sights in camouflage safari wagons with a smooth-talking guide who knows all the right jokes because he's told them before... and then back to the hotel for drinks. I am tired of the souvenir kiosks and the urgent encouragement to buy, to do a deal; the trophy taken home where it gathers dust feeling slightly embarrassed and out of place. And I am fortunate to have a wife who feels the same; we want to go where the water does not have a beer tin rusting on the bottom and floating plastic from previous tourists; sleep on an island in the Okavango that has no footprints on it, laying our sleeping bags under the stars and listening to the nocturnal cries of Africa.

And so the arranged boat trip. We met Myros' contact and he led us along dusty paths to his village, showed us his mother's home, his wife and his child. Children gathered about Gareth and walked with him, holding his hands.

Would we like him to organise some lunch of fish and rice for when we got back? the fisherman asked.

It sounded good; but when he suggested supper too and perhaps some local dancing I realised that we were still in the cycle of the tourist trap - not in the centre, the hotel and its squeaky-clean environs, but still there.

"No, please!" I begged, thinking of bored women donning their 'traditional' dress to perform yet again before the gawking tourist who would snap a few pictures and think he had observed a genuine local custom. It makes me think of period villages where employees are paid to wear historical costumes for tourists to gawk at, or the reconstruction of a castle or a ship 'just as it was'. I'd rather see the broken-down stones of a castle and know that they were actually *there*, than a modern reconstruction, perfect in every detail. I want to stand on the stones soldiers of old stood on, see the jewellery the people actually wore - tatty and cheap it might be - rather than buy the shiny stuff, polished for the tourist.

Anyway, we went and it was good. Three ragged fishermen with bare feet paddled us grunting against the wind in a choppy sea to the island. The boat slapped water about our feet and a baling tin clanked. Our guide felt himself slightly superior and paddled ineffectually; the others grunted as they worked, their muscles taut as wires.

On the island we walked over the rocks and through the under-brush, disturbing hundreds of gannets which roosted on the trees and rocks and splattered everything white with their dung. The rocky, overgrown surface smelt damp and ratty like the bats' cave. Large monitor lizards slithered into cracks as we passed; and once we paused to allow a bright green snake about one and a half metres long to pass. Then, on the other side, we stripped off and swam in the cool, clear water and looked at the tropical fish, striped and electric blue, which populated the rocks. Then a hard paddle back against the rising wind, the swells quite large and slapping spray.

Our fish lunch, in an enamel bowl of rice with fried tomato, was served under a tree. We ate with spoons and shared our food with the flies.

Back at the camp, Gareth's bike wouldn't start; it took us most of the afternoon to discover the fault - water in the points housing - and cure it. Almost dark, we plunged once again into the warm water of the lake, then ate supper of soup and samosas with a pineapple for dessert. Later we went to sleep to the sound of rain falling on the tent...

WEEK 3

Day 15: Tuesday 28 January 1997

(4055km 20%)

We were packed up and away by 9:00am. The road was good - narrow with many small bridges, most of whose railings were down. It wound its way in great sweeps through hills covered in bush, a delight for the motor cyclist, leaning hard this way and then that, a gusty wind blowing from the front and one side. We stopped and bought mushrooms - R1.25 for a huge bowlful of smooth-skinned, pale brown ones the size of a closed fist. The seller, a powerfully built young man with a sweet smile, emptied nearly as much again into our bag and I paid him more than he asked. He hadn't expected it - the extra mushrooms were a gift. I didn't feel obliged to pay more - it was my gift. We smiled at each other and it felt good.

Later we bought bananas and some dumpling things that children carry about in large enamel bowls. We ate the dumplings with syrup for lunch on a deserted stretch of beach near some fishermen's houses. Eating local is very cheap: dumplings, four for R1.00, a complete meal. Bananas, R1.25 a bunch; mangoes, 25c each; pineapples, R1.25 each; small local loaves of bread, 25c each. The locals make little piles of produce - tomatoes or peanuts or fish or mushrooms - each at a fixed price. They don't bargain and they refuse to split a pile. If you won't take the whole pile, so be it. But there is none of the sullen indifference, the masticating stare one so often gets in some countries. Here there is always a greeting, a shake of the hand, the wish for a safe journey that seems to carry some conviction. Gareth and I have walked through a jungle of the village market, surrounded by local people and shuttered in by stalls and not for a single moment have we felt insecure or threatened. It is only in the tourist resorts that one feels the need to clutch one's wallet and, so far, only in South Africa that I have felt in fear of my life.

In the early afternoon we reached Nkhata Bay and asked about accommodation. We were directed to two guest houses with dark unpainted corridors, bare rooms and half dressed locals lounging over balconies. We didn't like the look of them so moved on. Eventually we were directed to Africa Beach. I was dubious, expecting another pseudo tourist trap. But when we got here I was immediately entranced: lop-sided cabins made of reeds straggle down a steep slope to the water's edge. The bay curves round to the right where there is a quaint fishing village and a wharf. Dug-out canoes paddle the waters not plying tourists, but fishermen. There is no hotel in sight, no souvenir stall. Rickety board walks made of bits of driftwood, planks, poles - whatever is to hand - lead from one cabin to the next. A half-completed jetty, as rickety as the board walks, extends into the waters of the lake.

The rooms are roofed with a tangle of grass and black plastic; the walls are of reeds, the floors rough planks. I dropped some money and it fell through the gaps onto the rocks below. The owner is a local Malawian; he issues no receipts - just your name and how much you have paid in a book: R15 per room per night. A radio plays country and western music and the Cokes are cold. I pay for two nights, hoping we will stay for three.

It is a place of hippies and drop-outs; a place of dagga and free love and the meeting of travellers. Young men with dreadlocks and beads, with long hair like dissolute Christs, and young women whose navels curl tightly in their brown flat stomachs. A place for people with few possessions and less money and much time. With a shrug they will leave tomorrow and go to Zanzibar or Timbuktu or Khartoum for a whim. It is a place one expects to meet a Hemingway or a Graham Greene drinking at the bar.

Gareth and I followed the lake edge to the village. Men were bathing, washing their smooth brown skin in the lake water, unconcerned at our passing. In the village, rather dry-looking fish had been laid out in little piles - all small, from the tiniest the size of a match stick to the biggest, only match-box size. Everything stank of fish. On a large piece of plastic, a man was cutting up what looked like a goat. The flies showed interest. In the market we bought tomatoes to eat with the mushrooms and some peanuts in their shells. Then, the final touch, in sailed the weekly ferry which plies the lake. She was a gracious old lady, once white, now bleeding rust from every aperture, dirty and tatty like an old tart gone to seed, but she still carried herself well. Three decks, straight funnel, round stern and curved bow, she must have been built in the 1930's; she made me think of Nile steamers and flying boats and Conrad bumming about the South Seas in tramp steamers.

Later that afternoon as the sun was setting, she let off a blast of her hooter which echoed across the bay and, regally, as if she didn't know she was old and beyond it, sailed out into the darkening waters of the lake.

As evening approached and time seemed to slow, Gareth and I sat on the jetty and listened to the lapping water, reggae music from the bar and lonely shouts coming from the village on the still air. In front of us some fishermen, with the timeless patience of their kind, still tried their luck from dugouts on the still dark water...

Day 16

A glorious calm, windless day. We spent the morning servicing the bikes, then swam in the lake. The beach is clean white sand, rapidly shelving so that, about 20m out, we cannot touch bottom. Lunch of dumplings and syrup - the locals call them *'manyasa'* - and then a somnolent read in our ragged thatched huts followed by another swim. I could get used to this life.

Later we stripped the bikes down and gave them a good check over for the road ahead then we walked into the village and found a diminutive tailor, his bones protruding through a thin covering of flesh, white bristles sprouting from the dark skin of his face, to sew up the holes and rubs in our tent. He worked patiently in the cool of a verandah with his treadle Singer while the bustle of the town passed in front of him. Once back at the hut, we coated all the seams of the tent with silicone rubber to try to stop the annoying leaks and so we don't get flooded in Equatorial Africa. It looks ugly, but rather an ugly dry tent than a pretty leaky one.

Then another swim and a read.

Day 17

Woke late; breakfast of toast and honey.

A rest day, most of which we spent taking a long ride from Chikane Bay, following paths and tracks through the coastal undergrowth and trees from small settlement to small settlement. Eventually the tracks led us down the escarpment via a steep rocky path and onto the beach were we rode following the dunes and contours of the water for about five kilometres. Eventually steep banks forced us up the beach where the sand was very soft and both Gareth and I bogged down. We managed to free ourselves and battled along, the bikes revving hard and, even though unladen, ploughing *through* the sand instead of over it. With overheating engines, we stopped next to a high rock overlooking the lake and rested while they cooled. Then inland again, following narrow paths until we reached a large plantation of rubber trees being tapped for their latex.

Back at Chikane Bay we spent some time with a young German couple who had bought an ex-army three-ton Hanomag truck and travelled through from Germany to Libya, Egypt, Ethiopia, Kenya. We spent a long time pouring over their Michelin maps, trying to decide on a route north:

Nairobi - Ethiopia - Eritrea - Egypt - Libya - Algeria or

Nairobi - Ethiopia - Sudan - Libya - Algeria or

Nairobi - Zaire - CAR - Nigeria - Niger - Algeria or

Nairobi - Sudan - CAR - Nigeria - Niger - Algeria

Each route has its plusses and its minuses; each is dangerous because of war or soft desert sand or administrative red tape. It's an interesting concept: in front of us, laid out on the grass, the map of Africa; and from Nairobi one can go there or there or there or there. The decision is open. Nothing to *force* us in any direction. We could even, if we wanted to, head back to South Africa, sell the bikes and fly over. There is a delicious sense of freedom attached, a sense of having the world to explore and time enough to do it. As far as the route goes, we'll just keep on praying and asking fellow travellers and see what transpires...

In the early evening a strong wind blew up from the north and gusted through the bamboo slats of our walls. Gareth went for a last swim in the lead-grey water. Thunder rumbled and I watched two men paddle a dugout against the wind and the choppy swell, going purposefully somewhere.

Tomorrow, sadly, we leave this place.

Day 18

Last night one of the campers fell very ill. I offered our first aid kit. The ambulance was called.

All was a little mysterious.

The ambulance didn't come (it's Africa) so eventually a group of us carried him out on his mattress; he was as stiff as a dead person, arms locked as if embracing someone, eyes open and staring and periodically he twitched in a most dreadful way. I have very little doubt that it was a drug overdose.

This morning he is still comatose. The bohemian lifestyle is not always an easy one.

A Zambian truck driver told us last night while we sat together around a bare table on the verandah, "If you take tap water from one country and, as soon as you have crossed into the next country, you mix it with local tap water and drink it you will never get malaria." He has been driving his truck around Zambia, Malawi, Tanzania, Mozambique and South Africa for years and has never had malaria yet. Maybe we should try it. So far we have met two fellow travellers - one in Vic Falls and one in Malawi who, despite prophylactics, have contracted this unpleasant disease.

A lazy start this morning after we woke to a clear, still and very hot day. By the time the bikes were loaded we were dripping with sweat. Our arms and noses are burned but the rest of us is still quite pale. The road is badly pot-holed, but winds its way between bright green hills dotted with toadstool huts, all with their ragged fringe of untrimmed grass roof. Red-hot coals of bishop birds are startling in the grass; the road is often cluttered with scrawny yellow dogs with curled tails, men on bicycles, women carrying galvanised buckets of water, hands of bananas or a local type of spinach on their heads and a child tucked in a blanket under the arm - much better than the South African way of tying the child on the back, because at least the Malawian babies are able to see where they are going and take an interest in the passing parade. Along the sides of the road are stalls of bananas, very occasionally mangoes (the season is almost over) as well as large tables on which desiccated cassava is dried. This has a pungent sour smell which wafts over us as we pass. Some of the narrow bridges are overlaid with planks, first crosswise and then two strips lengthwise for the cars' tyres. But there are often gaps in the longitudinal planks wide enough to trap a motor cycle tyre and have us over. Few of these bridges have intact railings.

Then we reached the highlands and the road wound its way between high green hills, a brown swollen river following first this side and then that. At the top of an escarpment we paused to look out over the lake, pale blue near the shore but deepening to a dark purple near the centre; in the distance, a pale violet, the hills of Tanzania. We wound our way down to a small village which shimmered in the heat and, desperately hot, we followed a footpath to the lake shore, stripped off and swam.

Afterwards we ate a few bananas and oranges, had a conversation with three little boys on their way home from school who had stopped to watch us, and then were off again.

Then the turn off to Livingstonia, a Presbyterian mission founded by the Free Church of Scotland in 1894. Eight hundred metres above the level of the lake was the flat top of the plateau. A rough dirt road wound its slow switchbacking way up for 14km. We finally reached the top with very hot engines and made our way to the Stone House, an early mission house overlooking the mountains and the lake. About eight other travellers here but, sadly, the verandah where we now sit resting is lined with at least ten of the local youth who have decided to entertain themselves for the afternoon by staring at us.

Day 19

This beautiful stately old building, the Stone House, original home of the founder of the mission 80 or so years ago, is falling apart from neglect. When I ask the locals in charge why there are no lights in the bathroom or why there is no hot water, I am given the usual response: "It is broken!"

"And when will it be repaired?" I insist, feigning innocence.

My reply is a blank stare.

A Canadian and his English wife who have thrown up their jobs for a 5-month world tour share the house with us; as do two Norwegian men, a Dutch couple and an Irish man with his English wife. "Ah, rice!" the Irish man says, glancing at his plate. "Yesterday I was rather loose -" indicating his stomach, "- but now I am firm again!"

Of course we share anecdotes around the supper table, advice about the route ahead and behind. This bush telegraph amongst travellers is such a help. Now that we are nearly a quarter of the way through the trip, it is good to be included and to be able to share information with others about the good and bad of our route.

A breakfast of pancakes and tea but, predictably, there is no milk, no butter and no syrup. "It is finished," is the explanation, uttered with a resigned upturning of the hands. Fortunately, amongst us, we manage to dig out all three from our combined luggage and eat well.

Finally Gareth and I set off quite late after getting a little fuel from a 44gal drum.

We were taking a back road not marked on the main map, to Rimpi, where we could branch off and head to the top of the Nyika Plateau. What a delightful day we have had. The road started off very rocky and we were averaging about 17kph, but then, as the land became flatter, it smoothed out into a sandy track, smooth and undulating through and around the valleys. The road tempted us to speed and we were racing along at 70kph, keeping a careful eye out for water-filled holes, dips where the rain had washed out small gullies across the road, and sharp corners which sprang at us out of nowhere. The riding was exhilarating, like a fun-fair ride which lasts hours instead of minutes. However, the inevitable happened and, in a muddy patch I struck a channel, the bike slewed, struck another dip and I was off.

I saw it coming so managed to slow and then, at the last minute, hop nimbly off the bike as it went down so no damage to me or the bike was done. We had a good laugh! After 80km of this delightful road we reached Rimpi, filled both tanks and jerry cans, tried unsuccessfully to buy bread and change money then headed out along the Nyika Plateau road.

This was an interesting experience because for the first time on the trip I was 90% laden with almost full jerry cans (40 litres) and the road in very poor condition. We travelled at times at walking pace, paddling the bikes along with our legs through muddy ruts. A great strain on the forearms and shoulders because of the heavy weight behind, but we made steady progress. The day was overcast and cool, and it was exciting riding - very remote and challenging. This is what we had come to Africa to experience, narrow sandy and muddy roads, rural people, mountains and long grass all about us. I thanked God for the joy of living. Only once on this stretch did I drop the bike while trying to cross a muddy rut, but I managed to right it myself, despite the slippery mud underfoot and the full load.

Lunch of samosas and a pineapple on the side of the road and on again, along dry sandy and sometimes rocky roads which wound gently ever upwards. Again tempted to go a little too fast, I misjudged the shoulder, slipped on the loose stones and down I went again. Much laughter from Gareth, despite or because of a huge rip in my jeans exposing my bum. I think I will have to blame my heavier load, carrying the two 20-litre jerry cans full of petrol - I've come off three times and Gareth hasn't fallen yet. Fortunately again I anticipated the fall and got my wrenched knee out of the way in time.

At last the park gates: 86km to the camp. We followed the track ever upwards onto the plateau which is awe-inspiringly beautiful. 2000m high, it is gently undulating and covered with grass and bracken. In places it is park-like, in others more like Lesotho without the rocks. Deer of various kinds bounded away then, after a few metres, turned to look back at us. The air was still and chilly because of the altitude and, although it is the Nyika rainy season, blue sky showed through a pale covering of cloud.

We reached the main camp site at 4.30pm having covered just 190km in seven hours of riding. Typically, no one was around reception; the 'shop' was a glorified pub where all the workers were sitting around drinking. They were clearly the worse for wear and decidedly belligerent so we thought it wise to leave before anything unpleasant happened. We found the camp site and set ourselves up in one of their pre-erected tents on a concrete base with two made-up beds and a small table. Very cosy. Then we collected wood and will have our first fire on the trip so far.

Day 20

I have said some bitter things about Africa over the past few days, and yet last night we experienced that other side of the continent that so surprises and touches one. Sitting in front of a roaring fire last night, watching a dark cloud flicker with lightening in the distance over Zambia, a local man approached us and, using broken English and sign language, offered us three beautiful 10-inch trout. He is the watchman of the camp; he had caught them in the river during the afternoon, he said, and he had enough for himself.

We invited him to sit at our fire which he did for a short while and then quietly left. A very special moment, especially as we had just commented on the fact that we had nothing at all for breakfast and would ride on empty stomachs until lunch time. Now we have trout for breakfast. Gareth, I am sure, is a little concerned that we are lingering in Malawi. I think he wants kilometres of northerly direction under our tyres as fast as possible. I thought about this and explained to him: a) we are healthy b) the bikes are going well c) we are exactly on budget and d) we are happy. What a pity it would be to rush across the continent and then kick ourselves for not seeing more of the countries we pass through. We will have spent ten days in Malawi and what wonderful days they have been. I'd love to bring Glyn here on a holiday one day.

Today was a hard day riding, but a wonderful one. We rode for nearly eight hours covering 200km. I am writing this on a Jerry can outside our tent in a little isolated copse of trees, an open plain of long grass in front and a mountain behind. So far no little faces have popped up from the grass and discovered us, although somewhere in the distant bush behind us we can hear the lowing of cattle and the occasional raised voice. The skies above are grey with cloud and there is the occasional rumble of thunder but it doesn't look threatening. Although it is Sunday, we discovered a market in Chitika and bought tomatoes, onions, four eggs, four little cakes and a bunch of greens so I will make a savoury rice muck-up for supper tonight and we'll have the eggs and cakes for breakfast. I could have bought dried flying ants but decided against it. There were piles of them in the market, wingless and looking just like desiccated biltong.

We both badly need a bath and our clothes are very dirty. Hopefully we can find a rest house tomorrow...

So, to the day: we got away at 8:00am after a delicious nibble of trout with salt and black pepper. The sky was almost clear of cloud but still cold. We rode away slowly, looking at the many buck on the vast open plains of the plateau. Then we descended and left the park. The short cut to Karonga and the Tanzanian border was blocked because the rains had washed out the bridges so unfortunately we had to take the long way round. The road was delightful, same as yesterday, with our seeing only five 4X4's in the two days and 400km of travel, all locals. The countryside we are passing through is delightfully rural and isolated. And then I hit a piece of black mud on the track, the bike travelled sideways for about 5m and I was down, facing almost the way I had come. Gareth laughed like a hyena. No damage to me but the rear left indicator was broken.

Later we hit patches of soft sand as the road had become the bed of a river for the duration of the rainy season. I fell another three times during this exhausting but exhilarating day, just slow slides in the soft sand and over the bike would go. Gareth has hardly come off the whole trip. I'd like to blame it on my tyres, the weight I'm carrying - but I'm sure he just rides better.

After lunch we swapped bikes. I didn't fall again - nor did Gareth, but the roads were much better...

Quite seriously, though, Gareth has a natural relaxed style of riding which is a pleasure to watch. He has an eye for the right line and a sense of balance which makes the most difficult terrain look easy. No froth and bubble, winding it up, legs flailing and wrenching at the handlebars. He's a long distance rider, not a sprinter, steady fairly rapid pace. In fact he rides all day so calmly that I often wonder whether he has dozed off. What is he thinking about? Girls? I doubt it. The future? The countryside we are passing through?

(I asked him. "My mind's blank," he said, smiling.)

I sometimes get bored and swing the bike across the road in a series of wide S's, but I've never seen Gareth do it. He rides with a stoical imperturbability. Strangely odd young man that he is.

The bikes are still going well. They putter along at slow revs - usually about 2,500 - and when the engine is working up a hill you can hear each detonation, solid and strong and reliable. And then tapping off down a hill gives one that distinctive exhaust note of a large bore 4-stroke single. The bikes, quite literally, will go all day and feel as if they would go all night too if we asked them. We have a lovely sense of confidence in them now. Of course we ride with care, check them often and follow a rigid service schedule. Still, however, there are small niggles: Gareth's skid plate fell off yesterday with stripped bolts. It's quite vital because it shields the oil pipes from the front frame and under the engine, so we strapped it back on with cable ties and it is as rigid as ever but very noisy. My kick start lever started sticking at the bottom of the stroke today, but we moved the foot peg up a notch on the spline to restrict its travel and it seems OK.

Today I have thought much about Glyn and Jem. Being Sunday they have been at home and I have wondered what they are doing. Perhaps Jem has been riding. I miss them so much.

And now to my savoury mince...

Day 21

While I was in the tent cooking last night, Gareth noticed a wall of black cloud like a massive wave bearing down on us; it filled half the sky and blotted out the stars. In front, like foam, raced a line of white cloud. It was an awe-inspiring sight and, really, just a little frightening. We felt very vulnerable perched on the edge of our grassy plain. Realising that it would be upon us in moments, we quickly got everything under cover and battened down the hatches as best we could.

It announced its presence with a series of gusty flurries that shook the tent violently and then the heavens opened with a roar, the rain beating against the tent so loudly that we couldn't hear each other speak. Fortunatley, thanks to the siliconed seams, our tent remained completely dry. In fact, it was rather cosy, rice bubbling away, tomato, onion and greens cut up and frying in the pan and, outside, the thunderous roar of the rain. We soon realised why there was no one living on this lovely flat stretch of green grass - it was a swamp and, as the rain poured down, we could feel water rising under the tent; it was almost as if we were floating on a sheet of shallow water.

But soon it was past, the night calmed and we slept cosy in our cocoon of a tent. And then today dawned dry and overcast - another delightfully cool day to ride in. We set off across the grassy plain but soon found the bikes bogging down in a swamp of black mud. It took much revving, spinning wheels and paddling with both legs to get us through onto hard ground again.

The going was slow along rough sandy roads. After an hour we had covered a mere 23km. Then we came upon an upright barrier in the road. I passed through and was about to ride on when Gareth shouted. I stopped, puzzled.

"We've been here before!" he told me and in an instant my world turned 180 degrees. A group of smiling policemen confirmed it - we were heading back the way we had come yesterday, back to the Nyika Plateau! Now how this happened is a complete mystery to me. After our night on the plain we turned onto the road in the correct direction; we had come to no fork or crossroad and yet, after an hour of hard travel, we had ended back where we had come hours before the previous day.

A good laugh, turn round and back, this time with directions to a short cut which we found without difficulty - a 60kph narrow track of firm sand. At a junction we stopped for a short break and a direction update. On the side of the road was a small shop which sold warm Fanta, Fanta or Fanta. In fact, on her bare shelves, the shopkeeper had exactly five bottles of Fanta. Nothing else. We reduced her entire stock by two fifths!

Drinking the warm fluid outside surrounded by the obligatory crowd of children, I reached out to tickle a bare-bummed toddler's head but she screamed as if I had deliberately pinched her. Gareth said it was my looks that scared her...

It took us until 12:30pm to reach Karonga. Four hours to ride 130km. We were very tired and very dirty but we had seen something special of Malawi over the past three days, a rural countryside not usually seen. In fact, we didn't see another white person at all during those three days.

At the crossroad was a shop with eating place attached. I asked the owner what he had to eat.

"Rice -" the man said, then as an afterthought, added, "- with fish."

We ordered two and I went next door to get Cokes. A youth with dark glasses was sitting on the counter; he offered me dagga in a conspiratorial whisper.

Just then the heavens opened. Rain pounded down while we ate our fish - the whole thing on a plate, head with eyes, teeth, tail and fins, but delicious.

While we were picking the bones, an American man and three girl hitch hikers crowded in for shelter. The man was clean, the girls travel-stained like us. "Where you headed?" he asked.

"Wales," I replied, at last looking and feeling the part. No feelings of fraud now. We are seasoned travellers now and smell the part too.

"You can't," he said dismissively. "Borders blocked," effacing our trip with four throw-away words. "Wars in Zaire and Sudan."

I didn't argue; I was too tired and he was too smug and clean; only my resolve was strengthened to complete the trip regardless and prove him wrong.

The Tanzanian border post is made up of a collection of tatty buildings, leaning a little to one side as if tired, made of unpainted slats of wood nailed to frames. Inside, like most border crossings encountered so far, officials yawned and stamped forms, moved us from table to table, office to dusty office, where we fill in the same things on similar looking forms.

Where have you come from? make up any town.

Where are you going? say the name of the next large town.

Address? none. "Put home address," an official says. I write "Ixopo".

Stamp, stamp - thank you, have a nice journey.

The office for 3rd party insurance was a metal shipping container without holes for windows, but no one was there. "Don't worry," an official said, "buy it at the next town."

"But what if the police stop me?" I ask.

"No, they won't. They don't stop anyone."

Changing money on the black market is illegal, but if you lack local currency, the border officials send you to one of the touts who stand about outside with fists full of notes

and an amazing ability with mental arithmetic.

We are in Tanzania; we have set our watches one hour ahead. Steady progress is being made.

It is interesting that, although the borders of two countries juxtapose, there are distinctive and perceptible differences within metres of crossing the border. I noticed a woman riding a bicycle, then another and another. Bicycle riding for women seems to be socially unacceptable in Malawi; not so Tanzania. Here the trees seem bigger, the undergrowth thicker; the thatch on houses is no longer quaint but rather tatty, flung on willy-nilly; more corrugated iron roofs but mostly a dark reddy-brown and streaked with rust; many of the houses look like slum dwellings; brightly coloured sarongs worn by the women and toga-like garments over one shoulder worn by some men, regal and dignified. Toilets are provided with a tin of water instead of paper; the bricks used to build houses are bigger; spoken English is poor. Massive Scania buses with slogans like "Born to Suffer", "City Pride" and "Don King, Las Vegas" ply the roads with passengers hanging off the sides and even sitting on the roof. Whenever they stop, sellers converge by the hundred and cluster around the windows holding up their wares in flat baskets. Tall palms and banana trees nod and rustle along the roadside. And, amongst all this, there is a feeling of poverty about the land. Nothing I can quite put my finger on, but it is there.

On to a rutted tar road (for some strange reason it has been the practise to repair potholes in the road with red sand. This might be convenient and cheap, but after a heavy downpour all you have is a soup of red mud which disguises all the potholes - very dangerous if you hit one - and the whole job of road repair has to be redone) and on to the small sprawling town of Kayela, off the Dar es Salaam road.

Stopped on the main street of Kayela to ask for directions and, as usual, were surrounded by a dense crowd which pressed about us, hands reaching to touch this and tug on that, much murmuring and comment about us, the bikes and our equipment.

We were directed by a friendly shopkeeper to this hotel, bikes unloaded and pushed into a storeroom for safe keeping, we stripped off for a long-overdue shower and clothes wash. I trimmed my beard, then out for a walk around this fascinating little town of wide dirt roads lined with tiny shops and street vendors. The streets bustle with humanity, bicycles, goats and the odd cow.

The main item for sale on the side of the road seems to be bananas, from small ones the size of one's thumb to massive green ones about 600mm long (for cooking, we are told). Young boys walk about with flat baskets of boiled eggs and rough salt wrapped in newspaper. Because bicycles are the main source of transport (other than the humble foot) every street has at least four bicycle repair shops. We watched a man straightening a bent rim using his finger as a run-out gauge. The bicycles are robustly built and all have been adapted to carry the heavy loads they place on them. Extended stubs from the front axle support metal struts to the base of the handlebars to strengthen the front end; flat iron and even reinforcing rod carriers are attached to the back. Many frames have cracked and been re-welded. A one-eyed roadside tailor sewed up my ripped jeans and apologetically charged me R2.00 "because of the patch".

Having eaten very sparingly to say the least over the past three days, Gareth and I entered a street-side restaurant eager for a decent meal. We sat down at a metal table and surveyed the menu which boasted about 20 mouth-watering items. However, every time we tried to order something, we were regretfully informed that it was "not available". This is *so* the African way. Even if you have practically nothing in the kitchen, a restaurant must have a menu so a menu there will be - even if the items listed are made up. "Well, you tell us what you've got and then we'll decide," I said to the owner.

"Beef and rice -" he replied without thought or hesitation.

We decided on the beef and rice.

The cow they got the hunks of meat off for our beef was obviously too old, thin and sick to get out of the way of the bus that hit it a week ago, but it was an interesting meal served with a large bowl of rice, a bowl of spicy gravy, a bowl of cooked spinach and a plate with tomato and onion and a banana on the side.

As we walked back to the 'hotel' after eight, the town was still humming; bicycles with and without lights roared about the streets, bells ringing, every young man on his sports model cruising the sidewalks, out to impress the girls. The atmosphere is so vibrant and so foreign I felt the need to pause and open my senses to drink it in. The mood is unthreatening and often as we walk men call out: "Hello brother!" with no trace of irony.

Later, after we had retired for the night, I felt compelled to walk back out into the main street, alone, needing to absorb more of the mood of this small rickety town. The tiny shops were still open; street vendors sat in the darkness behind their wares or curled up in corners to sleep. I was invited into a 'restaurant' by a young man who sat with his friends on chairs on the pavement. The establishment - it was the young man's - measured about three by four metres; inside were two benches and a table. The doorway was partly shielded from the street by a torn curtain knotted half way, the rest of the frontage open to the street. In one corner, an upturned truck hub with glowing coals, an inverted half 44 gallon drum with pipe chimney to extract the smoke. On the table, peeled potatoes in a plastic bowl, five eggs and a gallon tin of old oil. I suppose eggs and chips was on his menu. Mosquito gauze separated the 'restaurant' from the opposition next door and I listened to the busy talk just audible above loud kwela music from a radio. I asked for a Coke and sat down. He fetched it from across the road. (In Malawi and Zambia, the caps of cool drink bottles are half lifted and left on for you to remove with your fingers. In Tanzania the cool drink is presented with the lid still attached and then opened in front of you, still leaving the lid on like offering a bottle of wine for inspection before de-corking it.) I sipped my Coke while the noises of Africa floated past me and thanked God for his wonderful blessings and for the joy of this trip.

WEEK 4

Day 22: Tuesday 4 February 1997

Three weeks on the road. 25.1% of the trip complete.

In preparing for this trip, I read a book called 'Smith and Son'. Published quite a while ago, it is the personal record of a trans-Africa trip just like the one we are doing. In the 1940's, Mr Smith as a young man rode a Triumph Cub from Cape Town to Cairo. Years passed. He married and had a son. The original bike he had kept in the shed, perhaps waiting for another trip, a sharing of his adventure, recapturing the dream. When the boy had become a young man - 21 in fact - Mr Smith proposed that they re-do the trip, he and his son, this time from England to Cape Town, following his original route. The young man agreed, another Triumph Cub was bought and prepared and off they set.

The tragedy, of course, of attempting to recreate a personal adventure is that it's never the same. It is impossible to expect someone else to relive one's own dreams or memories; it usually ends with the taste of ashes in the mouth. And so it was with 'Smith and Son'. It was clear from the start that the young man was not particularly interested, nor was he the adventurous type. At every opportunity throughout the trip he was angling to get the bikes loaded onto a boat, a truck or a train and, at every large town, would rush off to phone or post a letter to his fiancé. It was clear throughout that his son just didn't want to do the ride; had, I suppose, agreed to tag along just because the old man was so desperate to share his adventure, to humour him.

When the trip was finally over, the bike was sold. Reading between the lines, (although he never said it in so many words) Mr Smith was a very saddened man.

With this in mind, from the outset, I tried never to foist the trip on Gareth. I offered it, he accepted with his usual maddening terse equanimity and that was that. We planned it in a low-key way together, worked together on preparing the bikes. Gareth showed little overt enthusiasm for the trip (which made me sad) but that is his way. He really doesn't show enthusiasm for anything, which is not to say that he is not enthusiastic, just frustratingly reserved.

Now that the trip is a quarter of the way through, I know that he is loving every minute of it, just as I am. And I am proud that he has never shown a moment of weakness, of negative spirit; never a complaint, not even a murmur. We ride through blinding rain all day long and he doesn't suggest we stop or seek shelter or look for a hotel or give up. If there's food, we eat; if not, we don't - it's all one to him. We sleep on the ground or in a bed, wear wet clothes or dry - it is no matter. And yesterday, looking at the map, he said to me, "These countries in West Africa, what are they like?"

"Why?" I answered, non committal.

"I'd like to see them," he said... and my heart was glad.

Glynis and I, before we were married, tried to retrace the bicycle trip my father, brother and I did from Durban to Beira in our disreputable old Austin A40. That in itself was an adventure, but we couldn't capture the bicycle dream. That was of another time, resting in my memory and my brother's and father's. It can exist nowhere else. But *our* trip - Glynis and mine - became ours and new memories were created, very special ones.

In this trip with Gareth, I am not trying to repeat what my father did with me. It's a journey, an adventure all of its own, and if it creates in Gareth's psyche memories that will last all his life, if the time between us has been special, then it will have been worth while.

This morning, enquiring after a bank so we could replenish our money, an old man, thin and grey, gestured for me to come, wheeled his bicycle out of a store room and pointed to the carrier. Having observed the locals fairly closely, I placed my life in his hands and hopped on side-saddle. Off we went, his thin legs pedalling, tendons on his neck protruding through the skin like wires. I sat remarkably firmly and not for a moment did I feel insecure. Bell ringing frantically, we raced between pedestrians, other cyclists and the odd car, then along a narrow path through dark green mango trees and there, in front of us, was the bank.

With half an hour to wait before it opened, I ambled down a narrow lane shaded on both sides with tall dark-leaved trees, the ground littered with old mango pips and the husks of coconuts. In the yards of houses, women were sweeping the ground clean of leaves using palm-frond brooms; children played on verandahs and pigs grunted from inside their crudely constructed pens. Hens scratched and pecked contentedly, as always in Africa. Off to one side I noticed a crudely built-church. It was open so I went into its musty dark interior like the bat cave in Malawi, seeing the rat droppings on the floor, a yellow dog asleep in a corner. He looked at me disdainfully and walked out. But it was a *used* church. A blue-painted cross stood against one wall; the pews were smooth and crooked with use, and withered flowers stood on the altar. I paused, listening to the silence, and reflecting that, even in this small village in Tanzania, as in so many places throughout Africa and the world, using a hundred different tongues and styles, people were worshipping God. For a precious moment in that musty building, I felt a special kinship of faith and belief.

The bank was typical of Africa. I was the only customer, at least eight employees stood and lolled about behind the counter doing little or nothing (one ate a late breakfast partially hidden behind a jutting wall) yet it still took 20 minutes to exchange three traveller's cheques. The service was as disdainful as it was slow.

Walking back to town, I thought about breakfast. As if to order, along came a young man with a flat basket of eggs. I bought two - they were newly boiled and still hot - and he poured rough-grained salt into a torn-off strip of newspaper. A little further along, another young man sat over a pile of chapattis - thick, flat pancake things made from flour and water. I bought two and, back in our room, Gareth and I breakfasted on boiled eggs, chapattis and syrup.

We packed up and were on our way before the sun became unpleasantly hot. The road inland rose steeply to a plateau of 2700m, the bikes labouring a little and getting quite hot. We passed tea plantations looking rather scrappy and groves of banana trees watered by fast-flowing canals. The Chinese influence was visible in the Tanzam railway which followed the road, Chinese trucks and a mine sponsored by China.

At Mbeya, the owner of a motor cycle repair shop waved us over as we rode past. We pulled up and chatted. He sent a little boy off to get cool drinks while we looked the place over. In Africa it seems that nothing is ever thrown away; most parts are second hand and everything that can be is recycled. A worn sprocket was in the process of being re-filed into shape with a rat-tail file: new teeth, just lower gearing; a man laboriously rewired a stator using recovered wire from one that had burned out. In first-world countries the whole thing would have been thrown out and replaced with a new one or, if there wasn't a new one, a disappointed shake of the head. In Africa, *'n Boer maak a plan* and what ingenuity, what innate/learned (from desperation/necessity?) engineering ability! On the off-chance, we asked if he had an 'O' ring link. I was worried we didn't have one spare for deeper into the trip where they might be unobtainable. He rummaged in his pile of spares and *ta da!* there it was. He noticed my broken indicator glass and muttered to his assistant. A moment later, 2nd hand lens and

Phillips screw driver and it was on. "A gift for you," he said, smiling. It was a special time. Without a doubt there is a bond that links motor-cyclists in any part of the world regardless of race, language or social status.

After 250km and a dark threatening storm ahead, we stopped at a small village whose name I could not find on the map. "What's this town called?" I ask a passer by.

"Cald? Cold? Ah, beer? Soda?" His face lights up as he points to a bar down the road.

To escape the rain, we stop at a Guest House (Malawi has 'Rest Houses') called the White House, are shown two neat and clean single rooms by a young man who speaks fleeting words of English, but with appropriate gestures we make do. R6.00 each for the night. My room has a bed with a red and white sheet, pillow and mosquito net suspended from the roof; hurricane lantern for light, bedside table, curtain across the window, towel on a nail in the door and even a pair of plastic flip-flops under the bed for the shower (I have one green and one red; Gareth two blue.)

Outside, on the side of the road, a man strips the brakes and master cylinder out of a Land Rover with a shifting spanner and a few battered tools. We pause to watch. Gareth draws my attention to how much of the bits and pieces inside the engine are held together with wire (or *bhopa'd*, using the universal African lingo). I am sure that without wire and baling twine, much of African infrastructure would grind to a halt!

We unpacked and visited the stalls across the road, buying 10 mangoes, 2 eggs, 1 paw paw, 2 Cokes, 1 lemon, 2 rolls of toilet paper (all for about R8.00) and organised supper at the local 'restaurant'.

"What's to eat?"

"Rice!"

"Rice!?"

"Yes, and meat."

"How much?"

"400 shillings." (That's R2.70 per head - about 20p in UK money.)

Day 23

A day of extremes and contrasts. We breakfasted on a perfect paw paw with lemon juice and sugar, followed by the perfect boiled egg and toast and honey. It is interesting how a diet lacking piquancy makes the most ordinary fare in the civilized world a feast to the palate in outer Africa! - like a warm cup of soup after a cold day, a dry tent after riding for hours in the rain, a soft bed after sleeping on the ground, a friendly smile, someone to talk to...

The day began very cold. Even though we had descended the western plateau, we were still very high as we realised later. The land was flat, the road straight and boring. I wanted something to photograph, but there was nothing that caught the eye - just a dull landscape with neglected unpicturesque houses, scrubby trees (gone were the tall trees and palms just inside the border) and patches of stunted mealies grubbed out of the ground. Of note, though, has been the cleanness of Africa north of South Africa. One hardly ever sees a rubbish bin and yet there is no litter cluttering the streets, plastic packets trapped in puddles and fences and bushes like ugly flowers. And the reason is three-fold: firstly, packets are not supplied with purchases - you have to buy them, and they are relatively expensive; secondly, all drinks - soda and beer - are served in bottles not cans, and thirdly, the people are simply too poor to generate much waste other than the organic kind - excrement and pips and skins and bones, and these soon blend into the landscape.

On the road, men pedalled bicycles heavily loaded with 110 litres on the rear carriers of their bikes filled with bamboo wine, siphon tube attached. This was usually carried in one 60-litre plastic container, two 20-litre containers and another two of 5 litres.

Lunch of hamburger and chips at Lucy's cafe, Iringa, full menu and functioning. It was run by an Indian man...

We wasted an hour looking at a stone age site, 60,000 years old and supposed (according to the pamphlet, a tatty scrap of paper presented to us by the 'guide', an old man with one opaque eye and long yellow teeth) to be one of the best in the world. But, oh, what a pitiful display. In a shack latched with a hasp and staple pulling away from the wood, little piles of rock lay on the ground labelled 'flakes', 'hammer stone', 'scraper', 'axe' etc. They looked as if they had been randomly collected and piled there like tomatoes and potatoes on the side of the road. There were some that looked authentic and we stumbled across many more just like them on the ground, but any fool could see that most of the pile of 'flakes' weren't flakes at all, ditto the 'hammer stone', ditto the 'scrapers'. Run by the Dept. of Education and Antiquities of Tanzania - a sad comment. We foolishly left the bikes with all our belongings still attached and went for a long walk through a rocky and eroded landscape. When we returned we noticed that our bags had been tampered with and we are sure we disturbed the thieves in the act as we returned. Don't know what has been taken. Can't see anything obvious. We were lucky. Had we been away longer we could have been stripped bare. A very careless act which we must not repeat.

Suddenly the road began to descend. It entered a steep valley of natural bush and we must have dropped another 1500m and, as we descended, the temperature rose. At the bottom it was like riding in an oven or over the updraft of a fire. It was the hottest we have experienced on the trip, a frightening heat. What it will be like further north I dread to think. Fortunately clouds were massing ahead of us and we raced towards them, relishing the gusts of colder wind that buffeted us - and then the spatter of rain on our bodies as we reached the cloud. We didn't stop, didn't put on our wet-weather gear, just rode through the hot rain, feeling it penetrating our clothes and cooling our bodies... and we loved every minute of it! A small town/village appeared and we pulled over, looking for some shelter or a Guest House for the night but the usual crowd that surrounded was made up mostly of men who seemed very drunk and somewhat aggressive so we quickly continued on our way. The rain stopped and our clothes dried on our bodies within twenty minutes.

The land changed quickly to acacia thorn veld and, after about another 5km, into baobab country. We were riding parallel to a high range of mountains and the ragged landscape had become beautiful, the mountains lending the land a dignity that, sadly, the people in this area couldn't.

Finally we entered the little village of Mbuyuni, a squalid place, dirty and run-down. We had done our mileage for the day and were tired and hot so we stopped at the Mbuyuni Guest House as the heavens opened again.

Never before have I slept in a *khaya*. Tonight I will. The room is about as basic as one can get and lacks the cleanness and charm of our first Rest House in Malawi. This is a squalid dump. The doorways are low, up to my nose, so we walk about hunched. Through the metal bars on my window I can see into what looks like the local bar. The ceiling is stained, the walls had once been painted a dirty green (or was it blue?) and my bed has lost a plank where my hip goes. The shower smells of crap from the toilet, and said toilet - the usual hole in a concrete floor - is an egregious place, hung with spider webs from a rusty corrugated iron roof and stinking.

In many of the rougher urban places in Africa, one craps by squatting over a hole in the floor. In fact, even if a toilet seat is provided, often people squat with their feet on the bowl (with predictable results). This prevents one having to sit on the disgusting seat but the added height of the bum over the toilet leads to crap going everywhere. (This toilet, sadly, was one of those.) For me, with my gammy knees, this is something of a burden. Oh, the joy of sitting in comfort on a clean toilet seat moulded to fit the bum! Usually each 'toilet' is provided with a tin of water and no toilet paper. I suppose one washes one's bum with the water afterwards (and then, I assume one washes one's hands). But there is no soap. No running water. And *how* does one wash one's bum? There is no towel and, even if one were provided, I wouldn't use it.

I take my own personal roll of toilet paper, thank you.

It is getting dark now. Soon they will bring the hurricane lamp and, in its flickering glow, the room will soften and shadows play on the walls and mask the smudges and the spider webs. I will then wash in water that looks like weak tea, and we will eat our soup and toast and be happy...

Day 24

At six I couldn't stand it any longer. I got up, pulled on my sandals, and walked out into the pale light of dawn. The cacophony from the bar just opposite my stifling room was still going on as it had, without pause, *all night*. I had slept very little, if at all. Despite toilet paper rammed down my ear holes, the repetitive beat drummed into my head as loud as if the band was playing inside the room. Shirtless, I had tossed on my hot bed and waited for the dawn.

Outside, a few paraffin smudge pots were still burning, illuminating the sad little piles of tomatoes and onions, the fly-blown cooked fish, the stringy lumps of meat arranged on little stalls along the road for sale. I walked closer and something stirred. Huddled over behind the pitiful stalls were young boys, asleep. In the bar, a man was slumped over a table, yet the music blared on. And for a moment in that pale dawn I felt a touch of pity for these people - even young children - who, through necessity, are forced to man their rickety stalls all day and all night, leave the radio blaring and the lights on to entice a late-night truck driver in for a drink.

I walked out onto the road and away from the village. The bush all about was silent as were the overhanging mountains and, before the street came alive, it was strangely beautiful.

Later I woke Gareth and we tried to prepare breakfast in his room. I found myself walking about with my lip curled as one does when one's senses are assailed by an unpleasant odour. And suddenly I realised that was tired of the dirty walls, the grit under my feet, the rosettes of water-stains on the ceiling, the constant ducking through too-low doorways, the raw noise that assailed my ears, the greyish soup of water to bath, drink and wash dishes in, to sluice one's shit down a foetid hole, the unnatural squatting to void one's bowel, the shutters that didn't close, the mean passage outside my room which doubled as a drain, spider webs on the roof, rusted corrugated iron, blobs of fly-encrusted meat, the stench of fish and smudge-pots and blank faces staring. I wanted silence and clean, running water and a meal of something that wasn't dead donkey and rice...

While packing up, we discovered that yesterday, when we were looking at that poor excuse of an antiquities exhibition, my torch, Swiss army knife, dark glasses, my invaluable old light meter, binoculars and various other things had been stolen. *Bastards!* I muttered, just wanting to get away, out of here. *Bastards!*

And I realised that the tatty rural villages and flashes of the lives lived by the people might be quaint and picturesque when observed from the outside; but when one is *inside*, feeling the dirt and smelling the smells, battered by the constant noise and brushed by their bodies and stares, it is not quite so attractive. We were inside and we yearned, just for a while, to be outside. To sit at a clean table and eat a bowl of cereal with fresh cold milk; to drink a cup of strong coffee, sit on a toilet, bathe in a hot bath...

While loading the bikes, a man asked how I was and I angrily poured out my disgust at the dirty walls and toilet and shower and the noise. It wasn't his fault and my outburst made me feel small and mean but, at the same time, somehow purged.

Gareth glanced at me and said he wished he had a brick. He was referring to the noise still emanating from the radio in the bar. I must admit in the early hours I wondered whether I could sneak in and smash the thing but realised that my white skin would make me particularly noticeable and the reaction of the locals might be somewhat unpredictable. It was the second time in two days that Gareth had mentioned a brick. The first was after yet another bus had quite openly overtaken another in front of us and pushed us off the road. Gareth said he wanted to carry a half brick and lob it at the windscreens of trucks and buses that regularly pushed us off the road as they passed.

Once we were on the road, though, I felt clean again. I find that riding a motor bike does that to me, makes me feel clean and exhilarated.

The bikes were still going well and the first 100km ticked by. The hot, flat countryside had changed to mountains covered with green bush veld. Gareth was ahead of me travelling up a long incline between two mountains when I noticed puffs of grey smoke coming from his exhaust. It happened about four times and then, with a loud *bang!* and a flaming backfire, his bike lost all power and he pulled onto the side of the road. I was positive his engine had blown and had visions of the trip ending then and there.

Gareth, however, in his stoical way, simply took out the tools and got down to the job of sorting the problem. No *damns!* No wails; seemingly no emotion at all just, "Let's sort the problem out..."

"Please, Lord!" I whispered to myself. "Please, Lord -!"

We unloaded everything.

Gareth removed the plug and found that the electrode gap had been bridged with a lump of carbon. He cleaned and replaced it. Tried to kick-start the bike. No compression *at all*. (*What* - hole through a piston? Snapped rings? Riding valves?)

Remove seat, tank and tappet covers. Tappet gaps OK.

Now what? Still no compression. Would we have to take the engine out, on the side of the road, remove the head and look inside? Randomly, with nothing else to try before beginning major surgery on the engine, Gareth tried kick-starting the bike again - and it started! We looked at each other, elated and grinning. Switched off and tried the compression again. All OK - back to its normal leg-breaking strength. Gareth felt it must have been a piece of carbon causing a valve to ride.

Filled with a sense of joy and accomplishment, we replaced all the bits of bike strewn across the road, repacked and set off again. What a relief!

A very hot day again, like riding in an oven. Gareth pulled a strip of skin off his upper arm that looked as if boiling water had been poured on it. Sunburn.

We rode through the Mikumi National Park; the pure bush veld without people was somehow clean and refreshing to the soul. A herd of elephant walked slowly away from the road to one side of us...

The land became scrappy again, hot and dry and ugly, as if the soil was thin and poor. The effects of slash-and-burn farming were only too evident and the red soil was showing through.

At last, with the coast nearing, the air became cooler and there were some palms.

We stopped 40km short of Dar es Salaam, tired and hot and dirty. Booked into a better hotel - still shabby, though, like most of Tanzania, I'm afraid. The glorious cold shower in itself, however, was worth the price of the room.

Day 25

We are at Tanga on the NE coast of Tanzania, having ridden the last hour and a half in pitch darkness, Gareth with no lights at all and me with a dim, yellow headlight which did more to emphasise the darkness than provide illumination. We are physically and mentally exhausted, having ridden today for thirteen and a half hours and covered 470km, our longest distance to date.

In retrospect, was it wise? Probably not, but it is done and we are here...

The morning was decidedly unpleasant, heading into the suburbs of Dar es Salaam: dirty, sprawling, ugly and pinched, traffic jams and hooting cars, stares from the passengers of buses who looked down on us with undisguised interest. Dar is large and spread out, with 2.2 million inhabitants, mostly poor, most involved in some small business housed in a shack on the side of every road. We followed the main route through the city, trying to reach the harbour. I had hoped it would be beautiful, palm-fringed, dhows and rusty tramp steamers moored in still blue waters. Reality, however, was somewhat different: the smell of low tide assailed us long before we reached the harbour. No dhows, few ships and vast expanses of tidal mud and the filth that is usually associated with harbours. We stopped and I changed money, posted a letter to Glyn and we headed north, following the coast, eager to escape the noise and confusion of the city.

Gareth saw a motorcycle shop so we stopped, still needing a master link (the one we got at Mbeya was too thick in the lug and wouldn't pass through the links in our chains. It could, in an emergency, be filed and sanded to size, I suppose - in Africa, *'n Boer maak 'n plan*).

The owner, a sly-looking man with his eye on a quick buck, had a link which fitted. It was on a wreck of a bike which he said belonged to him. Thinking that our desperation would make him a good profit, he insisted on R75 for the second-hand part. I laughed in his face.

At that moment a young man who worked in the trade came in and he kindly took me under his wing. While Gareth waited with the bikes, this young man flagged down a mini-bus taxi and we roared off into the sprawling hodge-podge of shack businesses and began what turned into an hour of fascinating revelation. Amongst a labyrinth of dirty paths and roads, existed thousands of small businesses, many repairing cars and motor bikes (including a bike spares "shop" run from the back of an abandoned car!) - these masterpieces of 20th century technology with their entrails in the dust and shirtless men squatting before them making repairs with a handful of battered tools. And clearly, in their unsophisticated fashion, the repairs must be effective or the businesses would fail. But I wouldn't like one of these dust-mechanics to dip his dirty fingers into my engine.

We tried one motor bike junk yard after another, passed heaps of parts, rusting and unsorted. But the owners knew exactly where everything was. They'd dig down into the mound and emerge with a part, try it: wrong size.

Eventually, however, we located one - rather worn, but it fitted. Paid S2000 (R14), flagged down a bus back to Gareth, paid the helper for his trouble and we were off again, following the worst road yet on our trip. It was one of those roads that had once been tar but neglected until the potholes joined to turn it into a dirt road with hard lumps of tar and foundation sticking through. A bike- and soul-breaker of a road, dirty and mean and dusty.

At last, after 70km of this, we reached Bagamoyo, a fascinating old town on the coast with remnants of Arab, German, British and Dutch architecture and influence in its rotting buildings. The day was windy, and beached dhows fluttered their sails along a gently-shelving coast. Fishermen waded out onto the sand with bundles of fish strung through the gills with strips of palm frond. A young man tried to sell us coins that he'd picked up in the area, old Dutch, German and early Tanganika coins which dated back to the beginning of the century - a fascinating history of the area.

Enquiring locally, we learned that the road along the coast - another 200km of it - was just as bad so we abandoned it and decided to follow a small track north which joined up with the main road further inland. 42km we were assured. It turned out to be 64km, but what an experience! Very similar to the small bush roads in the Central Kalahari, firm sand alternating with soft, deep depressions, dry now, but judging by the radiating tracks into the bush to circumnavigate them, water-filled when wet. We crossed a river on a pontoon along with about 20 bicycles and 30 pedestrians, pulled laboriously hand-over-hand across by ten men who were not particularly concerned by the passing of time. The pontoon grounded on both sides, leaving a two-metre gap of open water between it and the bank; this made getting on and off the pontoon, with the heavily laden bikes, something of an adventure.

The soft bits were, again, exhilarating and - Glory Be! - Gareth came off twice. For some reason he struggled in the soft sand today, perhaps because he was carrying an extra 10 litres of water which he hadn't been carrying before, or maybe because I had empty Jerry cans and had re-tied my load to lower my centre of gravity. Needless to say, I thoroughly enjoyed seeing him flailing about and slewing from side to side, legs out, flinging up rooster tails of sand when he got stuck and, once, helping to drag him out of the bush where he had wedged himself against a bank.

We were tired and hot by the time we made it to the tar road. Low on petrol and with not enough to reach the next town, reluctantly we turned back and rode 37km to fill up. I bought some samoosas because we hadn't eaten for a while; after paying the young boy who was selling them to bus passengers on the side of the road, I carelessly dropped one in the sand. As soon as I had picked it up he approached me, gently removed it from my hand, and with a shy smile placed a clean one in the newspaper. This is the precious side of Africa and, almost without exception, it has been our experience on this trip. I was touched by his kindness and the gentle way he dealt with me.

But by now it was 4:30pm. 250km to Tanga - three and a half hours of hard riding. I suggested stopping at one of the towns along the way, but Gareth felt we could make it. Maybe frustration at not making distance north, I don't know, but I agreed. Although I knew it was unwise, I felt it important to support his initiative.

We rode hard and fast, racing the setting sun. Our bodies were aching, especially our bums, but we rode standing or crouched down behind the handle bars to change position. It was exhilarating stuff, pushing the bikes hard over good roads, keeping one eye on the slow revolution of the milometer while the other watched the steady setting of the sun, and all the while knowing we weren't going to make it.

It was sad to see, as we rode, the devastation the locals have caused to the land by a systematic process of slash and burn and the destruction of local hardwood trees to make charcoal. The lush bush veld we passed through yesterday in the Mikumi National Park has gone; in its place raw earth and stumps and the smoke of fires rising into the sky.

But racing along with the sun setting over our shoulders, the land took on a softness that it does in Africa at dusk, when the air cools and smells of warm earth and cooking fires and the dung of cows hangs in the air. The dust and smoke in the atmosphere became tinged a soft pink as the sun went down and everything was beautiful. I thought sadly of evening coffee and sherry in the bottom of an enamel mug and the crackle of a fire in the Botswana bush, the good times Glyn and I and the kids have shared in the past. Sometimes it is lonely riding within the vacuum of one's helmet on the bike...

But darkness was coming fast and we pushed on, stopping only after one hundred kilometres and then two hundred to quickly check the bikes. As it got darker, Gareth switched on his lights and I was consoled by that. I tried mine and was surprised to see a weak yellow glow. We stopped to don jackets against the evening cold and to remove our sleeping bags strapped in front of the lights when Gareth informed me that his headlight wasn't working. With my bike now showing the only light, I led the way with Gareth keeping close to my right shoulder, only slipping back when an occasional truck passed. Darkness descended and, eventually, we were forced to slow, 70km short of Tanga. We drove carefully and very slowly now, feeling our way in the darkness through an increasing number of small villages as we neared the coast. My headlight really only served to illuminate us so we wouldn't be run down by a truck (fortunately there was almost no traffic) rather than throw light onto the road. Passing shapes of people loomed out of the night like ghosts, and once I nearly hit a white-robed man walking in the middle of the road. Lights and fires partially hidden between the trees seemed so cosy in passing, with the smells of cooking food. Many times I nearly decided to stop at a village and look for shelter or even stop and put up the tent on the side of the road, but Tanga seemed so close that each time we decided to press on.

Exhausted, we finally made it by 9:30pm, asked directions in pantomime and were led to a wonderfully clean guest house by a young woman who walked ahead of us about a kilometre, with two beds and a ceiling fan, mosquito netting over the window, flush loo, shower. The owner, who speaks no English, gave us two cakes of scented hotel soap still wrapped, and that was luxury!

Day 26

A rest day. We stayed in bed until 9:00am, toast and coffee for breakfast and then a leisurely walk into town to enquire about a ferry to Pemba Island. Back in tourist land, the only ferry will cost R300 one way for both of us. We walked along the beach, explored wrecked boats and rusting hulks of barges, watched boats being repaired with an adze, logs shaped into planks to fit missing pieces of the large dugout outrigger canoes. The tide was out and the mud teemed with crabs and mud skippers.

Lunch of mango, orange, banana, peach and pineapple bought from the local market - delicious in the heat. Then a glorious siesta and, at four, a 20k ride out of town to visit some old ruins of a mosque. It wasn't up to much, but what was quite beautiful was a small fishing village we discovered by following a winding path through the bush. The tide was full and blue water lapped against a shore lined with palms; moored just off the shore, outriggers nodded against the swell, the water having flooded creeks of mangroves, making little dark blue inlets and islands. It was so tropical and so delightfully foreign that we stood and absorbed the scene for some 20 minutes.

Fascinating the moods of the coast: tide out, exposing the mud and smells of the shore, it is ugly; tide in, and the boats nod and rock on blue water - and it is beautiful!

WEEK 5

Day 29: Tuesday 11 February 1997

(Days 27 and 28 spent on Pemba Island.)

Home seems very far from me this evening and aloneness presses heavily upon me. Part of it, I think, is because we have made no northward progress for a few days, but mostly it is because this evening Glyn and Jem will be in our new home in Wales. They will be sitting on familiar chairs and sleeping on familiar beds while we lie on hard beds in a bare anonymous room, sunburned and tired. From the ceiling above, the clank and rattle of a fan stirs warm air about us.

The distance between us is still so vast: thirteen thousand seven hundred and fifty kilometres, in fact, and the worst still ahead. But I feel strongly confident that we will make it; Nairobi should be reached in 3-4 days and then the big decision: where to next? But whatever route we take, I just know we will make it.

We have spent the last three days on the island of Pemba off the Tanzanian coast. For some perverse reason, a fellow traveller in Malawi recommended we go there instead of Zanzibar so we did. And what a disappointment it has been. The ferry across was six times more expensive than the guide book implied it would be, but we needed a break and were looking forward to it so we went, hoping for tropical island beaches, clear water, uncrowded streets with stone buildings of Moorish architecture, veiled Muslim women walking by on silent feet and with averted eyes. We took our tent hoping to be able to camp on the beach somewhere remote like castaways.

What we got was a dirty, scrappy little island about 100km x 20km, poor and mean with no camping allowed, no beaches, the small harbour tucked in an inlet of mangrove swamps. We *had* to stay at the government hotel, an expensive dump of a place. That is the law for all foreign visitors to the island. In the "hotel" - I am reluctant to dignify it with such a term - there was no water from the taps, one light out of four in our room worked and the electricity went off at midnight so, after that, the fan didn't work and the heat in the room was reminiscent of an oven. Africa seems inexorably to follow Newton's 3rd law: everything is moving from a more complex to a more simple state. Fixtures are installed but never repaired: the ballast of a neon light fails, wires are taken from it to a bare bulb. The bulb fails, a lamp is produced; the lamp breaks, a candle is brought; the candles run out, a smudge pot is made from a Coke can; the paraffin runs out and you sit in the dark. There is no water in the pipes so you wash standing up in the bath with the water in a bucket. And whenever one asks about the lights or the water or the fan, one is looked at with a vague sense of amusement: do you really expect *all* the lights to be working? Can't you read with just the one?

But on the other hand we again experienced that other side of Africa, a special, precious part which I will never forget: people walking up to us in the street, "Hello, my friend! How are you? You are welcome here." When swimming yesterday at an isolated coral beach, a group of very poor men who had been spear fishing called us over. They gestured to a pot of rice, smoke-blackened, that they were eating out of. I dug out a small stale loaf - the only food we could get - and we sat together on the sand, communicating with smiles and gestures, and ate rice from the pot with our fingers, balling it into wads and popping it into our mouths and gnawing at the stale bread. That's all they had and they shared it with us, and I felt strangely honoured and touched. They had been fishing with home-made spears and home-made goggles - a piece of rounded glass held against the face with a cunningly fashioned piece of car inner tube fixed to the glass with wire. They had speared about six beautiful reef fish which they skinned (these seemed to have no scales) and held together with reeds tied through the gills. And the young lad a few days before who sold me samosas for lunch outside a garage. And a Moslem woman, African, with soft gentle features and pale satin-textured skin, breast fed her baby on the crowded bus, her head and neck swathed in yellow cloth which draped over her breast demurely. She looked like a Madonna and the pale undersides of her feet were tattooed with black curving patterns like the markings on a Samoan warrior's chest...

There was nothing to do, we had no transport, there were no shops open (it was Sunday) and all we had to eat was a very stale piece of bread and some cooking fat they sell for margarine in these parts. Eventually we managed to buy a cooldrink bottle full of dubious-looking honey, full of floating bits, which turned out to be runny and slightly sour as if it was going off. We managed to buy tickets for a bus trip across the island but, sitting pressed against the window and surrounded by a hot steamy crowd of humanity I became violently sick so we turned back. Finally, cutting our stay short, we managed to get a cheap trip back to Tanga and the mainland on a fishing boat whose engine broke down only once, leaving us bobbing and rocking on dark blue, flying-fish water with no land in sight. I got rather seasick, dipping and plunging on the foredeck just aft of the anchor, and the sun burned us both quite badly so it was good to get back to the hotel for a cold shower and a lie down.

And it was then, especially, that the loneliness came upon me.

Kenya tomorrow, heading north again...

Day 30

We left Tanzania after a pleasant ride of 70km along a palm-fringed dirt road. At the border, however, Gareth noticed that my rear tyre was soft. We pumped it and passed through the border, stopping about a kilometre further on at a roadside bicycle tyre repair 'shop' under some trees. Then began about two hours of dirt and frustration. Sitting in the sand, the sun beating down on us and about 25 spectators crowded around so that every movement required a body or a limb to be pushed aside, we unpacked, removed the chain and rear wheel then attempted to get the tyre off the rim which is almost impossible. (I think they design them that way to drive motor cyclists to the edge of distraction, sitting in the sand under the burning African sun in strange far-off places watched by a hundred staring faces offering inane and unhelpful suggestions. I am sure they do it on purpose to try to get normally clean-mouthed adults to swear most foully.)

We eventually got the tyre off, found the offending nail, removed it and repaired the tube, which had also been cut half through by the rim. The next task was to get the tyre back on without putting another hole in the tube. We failed. I have only repaired a motor cycle puncture twice and both times I re-punctured the tube when trying to replace the tyre on the rim. Most *sane* riders take the wheel to the nearest Supa Quik and pay the R20 - it's great value for money. "Please fix the puncture -" one says, and an hour later it's done. But there was no Supa Quik in sight, only a crowd of now even more interested and amused observers.

Well, despite vigorous pumping, the tyre was flat again. Remove it, patch the three new holes we had put in (five patches now) and do the whole job again (more carefully this time). It seemed to hold.

Through the Kenyan border and a pleasant 100km to Mombassa where we quickly found the Cosy Guest House. Filthy from our two-hour squat in the sand, we had a glorious cold shower and washed our clothes. A quick trip (meandering and lost, taking one-way streets the wrong way and dodging pedestrians) through the Old Town to visit Fort Jesus, a massive fort built in 1805 by the Portuguese and later taken by the Sultan of Oman. It overlooks the narrow seaway leading to the port of Mombassa and is massive and beautiful.

And then my tyre went flat again. What on earth are we going to do in the middle of the Sahara, dammit?!

Day 31

I write this in 'The Stage Bar and Silent Lodge'. There is a bar, but no stage is in evidence and definitely no silence. A radio plays non-stop local music from the 'office' which reverberates throughout the building.

We are now half way between Mombassa and Nairobi, 320km from the equator and have travelled 6,711km - one third of our journey. Gareth is making us a cup of tea while I lie on the bed, hot and exhausted.

It has been a tiring and frustrating day. We only got away from Mombassa at noon; at 8:00am I set off to sort out 3rd party insurance, change money and attempt yet again to phone Ted Russell who, hopefully, will be putting us up in Nairobi for a few days. I commissioned Gareth to sort out the puncture. After walking around fruitlessly for two hours, my nerves were frayed to breaking point. I am so tired of the noise, the bustle and bump of bodies, the refuse, human and organic, that clutters the pavement, the gobs of phlegmy spit where I put my feet, the incessant hooting of horns as never-ending streams of jostling taxis, conductors standing in the open doorways, attempt to attract fares. I have come to resent the pseudo bonhomie of touts, who attempt a fleeting friendship, establish a tenuous bond that kindles some kind of obligation and then the covert request for money.

The city seems to attract everything that is base in a society, the dregs, the petty crooks, those who prey on the weak; as well, obviously, as the desperate flotsam that drifts towards the city in the hope of averting starvation.

The phones didn't work - *lines* of them outside the post office, but not one would perform as it was designed to. Africa! My frustration grew. I purchased a very expensive phone card, but the two card phones were out of order. Finally I gave up and looked for Gareth. He couldn't get tyre weld so had dropped the tyre off at a specialist tyre shop to be repaired. We went to collect it, but, of course, it wasn't done. The owner, a well-spoken Indian man, said, "The tube is shot. You'll have to buy a new one."

I exploded, insisted on seeing it. Two of the 5 patches we put on the day before on the side of the road were leaking.

"Fix the damn thing!" I shouted, my frustration finally causing me to lose control. "It's got a puncture, fix the puncture. Don't tell me I've got to replace the tube - that's a special enduro tube, double the thickness. All you need to do is replace the patches. You're a tyre repair shop - *repair the damn tyre!"*

We stormed off to find some breakfast, secretly pleased that it was the patches and not further holes we had put in the tube whilst re-fitting but concerned at our inability to properly repair a puncture.

By midday we were finally off. The punctures had been fixed. It was a very hot day with the sun beating down on us from a cloudless sky. The land we have ridden through has been flat and scrubby, a dusty, ugly landscape, and the hot road went on and on with relentless monotony, no thunderheads, precursors of an afternoon storm to break the intense heat. The land was dry and wilting in this month of Kenya's lowest rainfall.

Then Gareth stopped. I rode back to him, fearing the worst. He was crouched next to his bike listening to the engine; it was knocking and rattling and the temperature was high. Oil has begun to leak from the output drive shaft or the oil pipe that runs behind it. My concern over his bike is renewed and I began to make contingency plans about how we could cut our luggage down sufficiently for both of us to fit on my bike if Gareth's gives up the ghost and we have to dump it. When it had cooled we rode on slowly, keeping to about 65kph. I looked out for Kilimanjaro poking its elegant snowy head above the clouds, but we were too far away to see it with any clarity.

After 5:00pm we called in at a garage looking for a place to camp: no, sorry, nothing, not allowed. An Englishman with an ex-army Bedford told us that all roads north are blocked. A German had been shot dead a few days ago trying to get through Zaire, he said. He even shook his head about the Ethiopia-Egypt route. But we'll make it, even if we have to hitch. There *must* be a way through.

Just out of town we came across this the Stage Bar and Silent Lodge - very clean and friendly, even the self-proclaimed guard who visited us in our rooms drunkenly. And now I have had my tea I feel quite a bit better. Nairobi tomorrow, hopefully a friendly home to stay in. And outside, the afternoon has cooled into evening and the loud music drums against the bare walls of the court yard...

Day 32

We are in Nairobi at the home of Ted and Andy Russell who are putting us up for a few days to gird our loins for the next big push, well aware that this 35% of the trip has been the easy part and from now on it should get harder. Just north of us lies the equator and we have 6,950km on the clock...

This morning I woke early after a bad night, noisy and hot. Gareth sleeps through anything. The discovery that one of the thieving bastards who crowded about us as we struggled with the tyre two days ago had stolen the radio out of my bag didn't help my mood. Unfortunately one thief taints one's attitude towards the entire society, unfair as that might be. And fantasies of catching the bastard with his dirty fingers on the radio and punching his face in swarm in my brain, a vicarious pleasure that frustrates more than relieves.

Anyway, robbed twice in one month. With at least another two months of the trip still ahead, that implies another 4-5 robberies. We resolve to be even more vigilant.

Our home-made pannier is cracking so I took it to a side-of-the-road welding 'shop' (man with welding rods and no eye shield crouched in the sand next to gas bottles) to be welded up while I bought eggs and bread for breakfast.

Then off by 8:30am to a lovely cool day despite an almost cloudless sky. It was so good to feel the chilly air on my skin again, that and the greenery of the countryside, the emergence of green-barked fever trees and some hills made the dry countryside almost pretty.

We travelled slower today - about 70kph - to baby Gareth's bike along. It will need to be treated tenderly if it is to make the rest of the trip. The road had very few potholes, but was bad - bumpy and amateurishly surfaced. Along the way we passed burned-out petrol tankers, a still smouldering burned-out bus and an upside down truck, the detritus of the Mombassa-Nairobi hell-run and local drivers.

We reached Nairobi at 1:30pm - a pretty town, clean and progressive and very unlike Dar and Mombassa. Ted Russell, who met us at the post office, said he at first thought I was an Indian, my skin is so well toasted by the hours of exposure to the sun. He had to work for the rest of the day but had a map of the city in his car which he lent us so that we could begin the sometimes fraught process of obtaining visas. With the aid of the map, we managed to locate the Ethiopian Embassy (closed), the Sudanese Embassy (no overland visas for Sudan *at all*) and the Zairian Embassy (border to the north still open, according to the receptionist). Visas only issued between 9 and 12, Monday to Friday so we will have to come back on Monday.

So, a door seems to have opened, but we are treating the Zaire information with caution. Our original route of Uganda, Zaire, CAR, Cameroon, Nigeria, Niger, Algeria, Morocco, Spain and France might still work. I am excited but fearful.

Last night Gareth and I opened our North West Africa Michelin map and fitted it to the Southern Africa map; our mere 7000km is puny indeed when measured against the frightening vastness of central and north Africa. We are, as yet, merely dipping our toes in the ocean that is Africa. My heartbeat rises considerably when I contemplate where we still have to go, the distances we will have to cover on bikes that are already old and showing signs of strain, and my concern for Gareth. I have become aware that part of me is secretly hoping that the Sudan and Zaire routes will be blocked and we can go the 'easy' Ethiopia, Eritrea, Egypt, Libya, Algeria route without losing face, but I know that if that happens, I will always be a little disappointed. I know Gareth has been very excited about the challenge of the north west route which shows guts. He expresses so little and is so reserved that he frustrates the hell out of me; but rather stoicism, I suppose, than a weak sentimentality or a shallow gushiness. He just takes whatever comes, good or bad, with calm indifference. I fear that one day he will create a great sadness in his wife and kids with his lack of overt enthusiasm, even though I know it is there, felt but unexpressed. Must chat to him about it.

Then on to the Russell household, a warm welcome and (oh, joy!) a cup of tea and cake; later (oh, bliss!) a cold beer as the sun set; then (oh, joy of joys!) roast pork with all the trimmings and a glass of wine, and then (oh, heaven!) a cup of good coffee followed by a hot bath and a clean toilet to sit on (not squat over) and a phone call to Glyn and Jem.

And now, to bed.

Day 33

A day of luxurious rest. Got up late, serviced the bikes carefully, relaxed and, during the afternoon, watched Wales vs France rugby. So good to get back to the normality of life after a month on the road.

Have been doing a lot of thinking about the route north from here. I have reverted to plan C after listening to the radio and hearing the news of the war in Zaire/Burundi/Rwanda: Tutsi rebels have taken the town of Isiro, just south of where we hoped to scrape through into Zaire. Furthermore, the Sudan air force bombed a town in northern Uganda last night which won't make things any easier. The Sudanese rebels not only control the whole of the southern border with Kenya now, but also patches along the Ethiopian and Eritrean borders as well. Although I'll check at the Zairian Embassy on Monday, I have spent a number of hours planning a route through Ethiopia, into Eritrea and then by boat to one of the ports in southern Egypt. Will refine this and check about visas tomorrow.

Day 34

Another relaxing day physically but a taxing day of mental turmoil as I waited for Glynis' phone call, just knowing that the news would be bad. It was. No job, money running out rapidly, bounced cheque to pay for the move, my old BMW 50/5 I brought to England with me in the move stuck in customs with no papers etc etc. This trip, which ought to have been such a once-in-a-lifetime adventure, is turning into ashes in my mouth. It now seems an ill-conceived and selfish ego-trip and the urge is upon me to head doggedly north ticking off the miles until we reach the UK. I feel physically ill with worry like I did at the start of the journey.

I don't for a moment blame Glynis for letting me know her position; it is important that I *do* know, but the mood of the trip has changed. The whole principle of letting the journey dictate our pace and not us force the pace on the trip must change now, but I must bear in mind the strain on us physically and on the bikes mechanically. Every puncture, every problem, every border delay or sign of sickness will now be a potential disaster instead of an expected and inevitable delay which, with patience and ingenuity, we would be able to overcome.

Anyway, despite this, I am still confident that our emigration and Gareth and my trip have God's blessing and that all will be well. I must cling to that and indulge in some earnest prayer.

Perhaps, now, in the light of this, it is better that we are forced to go the 'easier' route east. It seems that we should be able to leave on Wednesday, be into Ethiopia within four days and then straight through to Eritrea.

Glynis is worried that I will be killed and asked me to take out life insurance. I am convinced that it won't come to that...

Day 35

A productive day: visa for Ethiopia sorted out; visa for Eritrea tomorrow; managed to obtain the oil seal for Gareth's bike's final drive shaft and a proper master link for the 'O' ring chain, pannier re-welded and strengthened. Also managed to find a Michelin map for north east Africa. Our camera, unfortunately, is irreparable, the workings rusted from the wetting it got in the bad rain through Zambia. Then, when we collected the three spools of slides from the trip so far, it was only to find that about one fifth are totally ruined and three fifths over-exposed to varying degrees. Such a pity because the shots I have taken ought to have been good.

WEEK 6

Day 36: Tuesday 18 February 1997

Frustration! Collected the Ethiopian visas with no problem, then handed the forms to the Eritrean Embassy only to be told that the letter of introduction which we obtained from London is not acceptable. I must obtain one from the South African High Commission in Nairobi. After an annoying hunt though the city, eventually found the High Commission, filled in the necessary forms (asked for an introduction to the Sudan Embassy as well to save hassles later), but they said, "Come back tomorrow." Another day's delay.

Called in then at the Egyptian Embassy: good news and bad news. The good news is that there is no visa requirement. The bad is that our carnet *excludes* Egypt (a big worry to me all day). Our carnet must be validated for Egypt by the Kenya AA. Managed to locate this office, however the official said, "Can only be validated with permission from the *issuing* society. Will I please contact AA of SA and get it done." I managed to persuade them to fax for me. Call back at 3:00pm tomorrow and see whether there is a reply.

Anyway, at least the necessary documentation is being obtained, albeit slowly; and rather here in Nairobi (with English speaking, very civilised, pleasant people to stay with) than out in the desert somewhere at an obscure border. Just grin and bear it, I suppose.

Day 37

Glyn phoned last night. She sounded happy and chirpy which is good.

This morning I collected the letter of introduction from the South African High Commission, dropped off the documents at the Eritrean Embassy then next to the AA. The fax had arrived, but the South African AA has refused to validate for Egypt.

All roads north now blocked.

My devious mind working, I questioned the AA official in detail regarding the procedure required to alter and validate a carnet. He was most helpful and I paid careful attention. Ted, with whom we are staying, has lent me his Kenya AA card and, with little effort, I found a street rubber stamp maker (in Africa you can get anything made or acquired from anyone if you look hard enough!) and have ordered a duplicate AA Kenya rubber stamp for R40. I will validate the damn thing myself tomorrow...

In South Africa, a bare three weeks before we left, I discovered that the AA wouldn't issue an international driver's licence to someone with a learner's licence. This licence can only be issued to persons with a *full* licence. Here was the problem: Gareth is 17 and then still had six months to wait before he could get a licence - only issued after the holder turns 18. Without an international driver's licence, he couldn't do the trip.

There was only one solution: I had to forge one or Gareth wouldn't be with me now. Deep planning, my usually honest and law-abiding mind following dark and devious paths. I applied for and received my international licence but realised that it was too sophisticated for me to reproduce/forge. What to do? After a week of sweat, fear, midnight brain-wracking and earnest rationalising with God, I set this plan in motion:

With Glynis and Jemma accompanying me, all of us feeling that the word *criminal* was emblazoned across our foreheads for all the world to see, I made application for another International Driver's licence, hoping I wouldn't be recognised or served by the same lady who provided me with mine ten days before. We drive into Pietermaritzburg and make our way into the offices of the AA. Sit at an official-looking desk faced by an efficient-looking woman (one who would recognise me immediately for the criminal I am about to become). She seems pleasant and, unaccountably, does not notice my sweat or the trembling in my hands and voice. I am not recognised or loudly accused of nefarious behaviour. I hand over my driver's licence for checking - yes, it *is* me and the licence is valid and un-endorsed. I then fill in *Gareth's* details on the form, except for the first two digits of his ID number which reflects date of birth (obviously I do not look as if I had been born in 1979 - something this efficient woman could not fail to notice). I hand over the form, my heart beating in my mouth so loudly I am sure all can hear it. The official takes it and hands me back my ID book which I slip into my pocket and hope she looked at my photo and not my name or, if she did, that she has a poor short-term memory. She carefully copies Gareth's details, that I have supplied in place of mine, onto the licence and asks for my photo. I pass it over and she sticks it in and stamps it firmly with an official-looking stamp and then hands it back to me. I open it and memorise the position of the stamp and by how much it straddles the photo-edge.

Now comes the devious bit, carefully rehearsed: while I remain seated at the desk, Glynis asks to buy a camping torch from one of the shelves away from the desk. The official stands to get it and goes to the till. Nonchalantly, with sweat pouring from my arm pits, I reach over and pick up the official stamp on her desk. Gareth's passport photo has been all the while held against the palm of my sweaty hand with one finger. Without glancing around to advertise my guilt, I press the stamp against Gareth's photo in the correct position, overlapping just the right amount, then, just as nonchalantly, replace the stamp into its holder on the desk.

The deed has been done...

Outside, Glynis says, "No wonder so many people take to crime!"

Later, at home, I peel off my photo and replace it with Gareth's. It is a perfect fit. Judicious use of Tippex alters the 51 of my birth date to the 79 of Gareth's so the ID number is correct and we have an International Driver's Licence for my 17-year-old son.

I couldn't do it for a living, though. The fear and guilt would kill me.

Gareth and I spent the afternoon and night with friends on a coffee plantation near Thika. A lovely old early colonial-style farmhouse shared with their six dogs. The few ex-pats we have met in Kenya live a good life. The frustrations of Africa are accepted with wry tolerance and a "what would you expect?" attitude, but they isolate themselves as best they can and have their servants (2-4 per household), the sunshine and a relaxed pace of life. But many of them also have their guns at hand for protection or a guard permanently on the gate. In Kenya the roads are bad, petty crime a nuisance, the electricity goes off every day for a few hours, but they plan their lives around it. At times certain basics are unobtainable in the shops, but they can cope; the corruption of politics, local and central, is noted with cynical complacency as the newspapers are glanced through (the so called "two minute silence"); racial comments are made with an "aren't we naughty" smile. And so, quality of life is weighed against the frustrations of Africa and found to be acceptable. There's no great rush to get away.

Day 38

After a relaxed breakfast, I collected the Eritrean visa, then picked up my street-made AA Kenya stamp. A work of art! What amazing talent - a negative image cut into an erasor with a razor blade and you can't tell the difference from the original. The Carnets were quickly self-validated with forged stamp and red pen as instructed, with a little prayer that all will be well.

Day 39

We crossed the equator at 1:30pm, passing through the Rift Valley on the way to Nyahururu. The day was cool and hazy so that everything looked as if it was somehow far away. It's a good feeling to be over the ridge, as it were, at last, and heading downhill to the UK.

Through the Rift Valley, the land falling away suddenly, the flat dusty plains stretching into the milky distance. The valley itself was flat and dry, almost semi-desert in places, suffering badly from the drought. Both Lake Naivasha and Lake Nakuru were almost dry - little more than white sheets of sand and chemical deposits shimmering in the heat.

As we reached Nakuru, however, it changed: the streets were lined with shady Jacaranda, frangipani and coral trees in blossom. While Gareth guarded the bikes, I bought bread and some "steak" for supper - hacked off a cow hanging from the ceiling in a fly-screened partition - and then the steep climb out of the valley. Suddenly there were trees, soft ones like flat crowns, gum and firs, the temperature cooled and we reached the plateau.

In the early afternoon we stopped at Nyahururu, setting up our tent near the Thompson Falls. There we met a young Danish couple also on a motorbike. They were wise - flew themselves and the bike (a brand new Honda 650) to Nairobi and are exploring East and Southern Africa for six months. Friends of theirs, they told us with glee, have just been trapped in Egypt for three months with bureaucratic hassles and had to ship their bikes to Syria and then Eritrea. Doesn't do my confidence much good with our forged carnet validations.

We shall see...

Day 40

I am sick. Bad diarrhoea and running a mild temperature. I didn't sleep at all last night; today I have plodded along on the bike with little if any joy. Fortunately Gareth is fine so what gave it to me heaven knows.

Last night we made a fire and cooked rice and the steak, which was so tough it was almost impossible to chew. And then, while Gareth was showering the old loneliness came upon me again, partly because I am not feeling well and partly because of the comfort of having stayed in a home with a family over the past six days. Then, of course, the worry about Egypt and the route north...

We rode today mostly along a high plateau which made the air delightfully chilly, Mount Kenya appearing in the milky sunlight on our right and getting more clear as we approached, a majestic, rocky, snow-capped peak. As with yesterday, the highlands are beautiful, clean and cool and green despite the drought. But soon we descended, the land flattened, the road turned to dirt and we struggled over 97km of very bad road, patches of bull-dust hiding deep holes that would catch us unawares and threaten to have us over.

On a very deserted stretch of road I saw one of the tallest termite nests I have ever seen and we pulled over to have a look. It must have been a good 18ft high and towered over us when we stood at its base. While we were looking, a group of two women and five children came walking through the brittle grass. They had been collecting firewood and the younger of the two carried a load of sticks on her back; the other had a child strapped onto her back with a strip of cloth in the African way. Even a young girl who couldn't have been older than 6 or 7 was carrying her younger brother. They were all bare foot and walked through the thorn-veld and dry spiky grass with no apparent discomfort. The women were beautiful, their features finer and more in keeping with the Ethiopian and Eretrean women than those we had encountered further south. Despite - or perhaps because of - the harshness of their lives in this semi-desert region, they were all in excellent health and carried their bodies with an erect pride. We conversed in sign language a while then headed back to the dirt road.

But we finally reached the tar again, missed the turn and had to backtrack 27km, then a final 35km to Isiolo, the jumping off point for road convoys which gather and travel across 550km of bad dirt to the Ethiopian border.

We booked into a guest house and I collapsed, leaving Gareth to sort out the arrangements with the police for tomorrow (all vehicles travelling through this difficult section of wild, partially desert bad-lands in northern Kenya have to travel in convoy, protected by the Kenyan army because of attacks from Shifta bandits who seem to have a ruthless and cruel reputation.) After the cool highlands, my room is like an oven and slow-flying flies trouble me. I am at a low ebb and know that the next two days are going to be very difficult. Such a pity that at this stage my health should fail.

Day 41

Today, physically, I came very close to the end of my tether. Partly I suppose it was because for the previous 30 hours fluid has been draining out of me every hour in the worst case of diarrhoea I have ever had. In retrospect it probably would have been wiser to delay and get my strength back, but we finally reached Marsibit (260km from Isiolo) in eight and a half hours, riding in the blazing sun over one of the worst roads I have ever encountered, full of rocks and corrugations and bull dust for the entire day; a bike-breaker of a road, a spirit-sapping road. But we made it (only half way, though: another 250km of the same to the Ethiopian border still to go).

We will rest up tomorrow, and tackle that section on Tuesday; we, physically, and the bikes, mechanically, need a rest.

At 8:30am we reported at the police barrier to join the convoy, but it had already left half an hour before. "But you can catch it up," a policeman nonchalantly assured us and then he tried unsuccessfully to get some money off me.

At first, as always, the road wasn't too bad, but that is usually because one is fresh and the world rosy. Physically I was feeling OK and even had tinges of the old joy of riding coming back. This was what we had come for: Africa in all its harsh rawness. The dirt road stretched ahead across a flat land with, every now and then, a massive mountain, pale blue and rocky, thrusting itself out of the ground. It was a starkly beautiful landscape, devoid of people or habitation.

And then we saw camels, a large herd, crossing the road ahead. At intervals along the side of the road we came across Samburu tribesmen, who wear a dark red toga-like garb and carry spears. Their faces are sometimes painted in intricate patterns of yellow ochre, their fine features set off with beads and silver jewellery, head bands and feathers. One could almost call them beautiful, but in a proud, masculine way. They were dignified and when I asked whether I could photograph them, they refused; one young girl, about fifteen, wanted to attack me with a fist-sized rock when I proposed a photograph along the side of a deserted stretch of road where she was walking with her goats. I got the message: no photographs.

On the road, our troubles started when Gareth fell badly, injuring his leg. I had lost a Jerry can which hooked on a high ridge of loose stones and went rolling across the road spewing petrol. (These longitudinal ridges are built up by convoys of trucks and, if one hits them at an angle, it takes all one's strength and skill to keep the bike from going over. In the direct sunlight before and after midday, they are almost impossible to make out and they blend with the dusty whiteness of the road.) Behind me, Gareth braked hard, unfortunately favouring his front brake; the front wheel dug in and over he went. He was up quickly but there was blood on his knee where his jeans had been ripped. We got the bike up - it takes both of us to lift a downed bike; one water bottle badly crushed and my Jerry can holed. Gareth stripped off boots and jeans. The flesh had been deeply torn away on his left knee and the palm of one hand. He accepted my ministrations with his usual stoicism. I bandaged him up and we headed off again.

At about 11:30am we came across a big bike, front wheel missing, propped up on rock, tools and kit spread about in the sand. As we stopped, a large man emerged from the shade of a thorn bush where he had been resting and flagged us down. He looked travel-stained and desperate. "You got a spare tube?" he called. We nodded and dragged out our spare front tube from inside our spare tyre.

His name was Carl, an Australian biker on a round the world trip. He had been riding with five other bikers - American, German and Danish - in a loosely cohesive group and was at the back, travelling at about 80kph, when his front tyre went flat. Somehow he managed to keep the bike up, found rocks to elevate the front wheel and had spent the last two hours trying to repair the tube - without success. He looked exhausted and frustrated but relieved that we had chanced along (with a spare tube ready to hand). You can't ride a bike very far with a flat front tyre.

The others hadn't come back to help him. He said a few words about his companions in choice Australian dialect, mostly beginning with 'F'. On his petrol tank was a formal-looking sticker which said:

WARNING

Remember to put fuel in the tank.
Try to wear a helmet.
Ride like a twat.

Australian humour...

He'd used up all his patches, he told us, taken the tyre off and replaced it about nine times (with accompaniment of choice language, I'm sure) and even tried to stuff his spare rear tube (18 inch) into the front tyre (21 inch) and had finally decided to attempt to hitch a lift with a truck back to Nairobi.

We quickly fitted our spare tube, replaced the wheel and we rode on together.

Perhaps it was my exhaustion taking its toll on my concentration, the appalling road and the weight on my bike, but during the day I fell three times, twice hard, ripping my knee open deeply and grazing my arm. Carl and Gareth bandaged me up; the blood and the shock of the crash had made me physically ill.

But we were soon back on the seemingly never-ending road, concentrating on keeping the bikes on the rocky but stable strips between the soft, dangerously treacherous ridges of accumulated pebbles, sand and bits of rock which the large trucks had built up. Gareth's brake shaft rattled off but we managed to find a bolt to replace it; not quite the right size but it will do; Carl's one brake calliper rattled loose and was lost, the aluminium mounting and remaining disk badly worn. We managed to fit a spare, with more lying in the dust and heat to repair it.

And as 3:00pm moved slowly to 4 and then to 5:00pm, I found myself weakening. I had difficulty kick-starting my bike - I was just too exhausted; the falls and the heat and the strain of trying to keep the bike up had taken a tremendous toll on my physical reserves. What was so touching to me was the way Gareth noticed and, without fuss, helped me, quickly offering to kick-start my bike when he saw me struggling. I accepted gladly. Two or three kicks and, if the bike hadn't started, I was almost too exhausted to lift my leg, especially with the heavy boot attached, let alone give the tremendous kick required to start the big thumper. I found that I was having difficulty holding my head up and every muscle in my body cried out for rest.

Then Carl's bike broke in half, the frame snapping on both sides.

It was that kind of road.

We waited with him, knowing that, for him at least, it was the end of the trip. He spoke about giving up and heading home. Fortunately, it wasn't long before a truck trundled along and the driver agreed to cart the bike the last 50km to Marsibit. We left Carl with a group of willing helpers lifting his bike onto the back of the truck and rode on.

A short while later we came across a group of German bikers on their way to South Africa. They had come across the desert and looked well travelled, their bikes heavily laden. We stopped for a while and traded information on the road ahead.

We finally reached Marsibit as the sun was setting, and checked in to the local hotel. There we met the other five riders: two Germans on a KTM and a Tenere, an American on a BMW, and a young Dane riding a rather tired XR500. (They were a little sheepish about their desertion of Carl, but insisted they thought he was in front and had ridden ahead. They claimed that Carl had only two speeds regardless of the road conditions: full speed or stop, and, from what we saw of Carl's riding today, I can believe them.)

For a long time I lay on my bed, exhausted, unable even to wash. But we have made it.

Day 42

A day of rest, of lying on beds reading and allowing our (mainly *my*) exhausted body to recover. I have no energy at all and can eat little. We removed the bandages on our legs, washed my deep cut just below my knee and Gareth's raw wound where the road literally ground away a section of his flesh, applied antiseptic powder liberally and bound them up again. We are both very stiff and sore and hobble about like cripples. We rested until late; Gareth made toast and marmalade for breakfast and then we found a garage to weld the cracked jerry cans, checked the bikes over carefully and cleaned the air filters. Then we rested until lunch. Rested again until 3:30pm then rode out - unladen for the first time - following a dirt track which wound its way through the scrubby thorn veld and the beginnings of desert dunes. Around a corner we came across a man leading three laden camels. It was a wonderful sensation: red dirt track, camels, semi-desert landscape all about us.

This was confirmation that we really are making progress north, really are in a remote part of the world, can now call ourselves "travellers". The semi-desert shael landscape surrounding us, the camels... Further on we came to a water hole with hundreds of camels being watered by local tribesmen. The vegetation had been completely destroyed throughout the surrounding area by over-grazing and it seemed we were very close to true desert. We got off the bikes, sat down in the hot sand and watched for a while, absorbing the atmosphere. Then, reluctantly, back to Marsibit where we loaded the bikes ready to tackle the next section of this horrible road tomorrow. We have thrown out one water bottle and Gareth has taken the tent on his bike to lighten my load, bless him. Finally we filled up with fuel, ready for an early start, if possible before the sun gets too hot.

Reliable sources say the road from here to Moyale on the Ethiopian border is worse than from Moyoli to here and only 10km shorter. We plan to ride slowly and carefully, caring for both ourselves and the bikes - the tyres especially because now we are without a spare front tube.

The group of five bikers are also leaving for Moyale tomorrow, but they travel much faster than we do so we will not suggest riding together. They plan to reach Europe via Saudi Arabia, Jordan, Israel, boat to Greece, boat to Italy and home. They are shunning Egypt because of its reputation for hassling overlanders. Despite my cunning self-validation of our carnets, my gut feeling is to do the same.

We will see...

WEEK 7

Day 43: Tuesday 25 February 1997

(8000km 40%)

I write this from my room in Moyale, Ethiopia. We are showered and clean (first wash with running water since Nairobi), our stomachs are full of spaghetti and hot chilli sauce (called *wat*); I am happy and fulfilled and at peace with the world.

What is interesting writing this diary day by day is that it reflects my mood swings with the immediacy of the moment, which an account of the trip in retrospect would miss. After an intervening gap of time one tends to gloss over the hard times, the despair and sickness, and only remember the highlights. I am finding that this trip is an emotional roller coaster, although now that we are across the equator, in a truly 'foreign' part of Africa (Kenya is still very civilized) and 40% of the way through, we are at peace about making total fools of ourselves if the bikes pack up, or we have to abandon the trip for whatever reason, as we were for the first few weeks. The bikes seem to have settled, although Gareth's rattles and clanks along, and my heart doesn't leap into my throat if I catch a hesitation in my engine or notice that Gareth has stopped on the side of the road behind me. Somehow, I am sure, we will make it.

Just which way we will go, though, is still a problem. I noticed today that our carnets exclude the Middle East and Greece. Back to square one.

Anyway, to today. Strangely enough, this day came close to being the best day of our entire trip so far. A joy of a road; a motor cycle traveller's delight of a road!

But let me start at the beginning...

We awoke to the mournful wail of the muezzin calling the faithful to prayer. It was still dark outside. I had not slept well, knew it was 5:00am and time to get up, but lay for another 15 minutes enjoying my bed and fearful of what the day had in store for us. Both of our damaged knees from the accidents had stiffened by the time we went to bed and we are very conscious of riding with no armour at all except for our boots. Our legs are vulnerable on roads like these and we are very far from help if something really bad occurred.

Finally I dragged myself out of bed and woke Gareth (as always he sleeps with the pillow over his head and simply cannot wake on his own) and we ate a breakfast of hard boiled eggs (bought the evening before) while we packed in the semi dark. Our ripped knees - ugly wounds, Gareth's flesh ground away deeply and mine ripped open and needing stitches - we bound tightly with all the bandages we have, trying to give protection in case of another fall.

The five other riders were also getting ready and, as we prepared our bikes together in the dark courtyard under the sleepy gaze of the night watchman, there was that feeling of excitement one gets when a child, waking up in the before-dawn-dark to prepare for a long holiday journey. By now Gareth and I are seasoned travellers (and have the wounds to prove it), and felt able to take our place in the loose camaraderie of the group. The others decided to wait for first light and to have coffee first, but Gareth and I set off on our own, anxious to get away and make the most of the cool of morning, knowing too that we would probably be riding slower and they would soon catch us.

As we rode through the dark deserted streets, dusty and littered, I felt the old twinge of joy I so often feel when starting off the day, the unique pleasure of riding a motor bike along little-used roads through a wild and foreign country, the cool air blowing against my face, the excitement of the unknown ahead. My body had recovered well and my stomach was fine. It was good to be well again.

And then a massive Fiat truck and trailer pushed me off the road; whether he had seen me or not I do not know but he overtook me in the dark and, before he was past, cut in. My dim yellow headlight showed nothing but the clouds of dust thrown up by thundering wheels within inches of my shoulder, the road was rutted and covered with large stones and thick ridges of sand and suddenly I realised that unless I took evading action the trailer was going to hit me. I swerved into the blackness on the left and into the soft shoulder, the bike lying down with my leg under it while the truck lumbered away into the darkness. So much for slow and careful. I gingerly picked my bike up and started off after Gareth who was some way ahead, unaware of my accident.

The police barrier loomed up in the darkness. Already about five trucks and trailers were lined up for the convoy. We parked and made our way to the police shack.

"When does the convoy leave?" I asked.

"Maybe 7:30, 8:00," the soldier said.

Bitterly disappointed, Gareth and I sat down in the dark to wait. Around us, truck drivers were drinking sweet black tea served by a woman with a child on her back. I wished she would offer me a cup. Already the sky to the east was lightening, but a cool wind had begun to blow clouds across the sky from the east - perfect for riding.

After ten minutes of frustrated waiting, we approached the soldier again. He told us that the Shifta usually attack about

6km down the road and he pointed to a hill in the distance. "But they won't attack motor bikes," he assured us.

"Could we go on ahead on our own?" I asked, looking at Gareth who nodded.

"Yes," he said casually. "Once you're past that hill you should be all right."

In a trice we were on our bikes and picking our way carefully along the dark road, hoping we wouldn't come across a line of rocks blocking our way.

We passed the six kilometre hill as the sun rose. The semi-desert landscape was beautiful as only it can be in the late evening or early morning. We paused to look into a large volcanic crater below and to the left of the road - an eerie sight in the pale dawn light and then on again, making good time on a smooth dirt road.

The land flattened and the semi desert turned into pure desert, rocky and desolate, not a blade of grass and only a few stunted and dusty acacia trees to break the stark monotony of the landscape all about us. We had entered the Chalbi Desert, the road was remarkably good and, as I rode, I thought, as I had done before in Malawi and Tanzania: This is what we came for. This is Africa far from the tourist routes, deep into the desert, a slightly frightening but incredibly beautiful place.

And then the five other bikers caught us and we stopped together for a break. The Germans lit cigarettes and Greg offered around a packet of dates. We ate together, sharing travel stories and discussing the route ahead. What a nice bunch they have turned out to be: Greg, a Californian on a BMW 1000, two and a half years into a trans-world trip, engineer, late 20's, impish grin; Torbin, a Dane, young (23) with a long fringe over his eyes. He speaks with a laid back drawl and smiles shyly. He rides an old rat-bike-ish XL500 which he bought in South Africa, welded a rack on the back and he ties everything on with ropes and straps. All the left-overs go on a frame pack on his back. Then "The Germans", two men in their late 20's and a girl. They ride a KTM 620 and a Tenere 600, both men tall and dark and big, typical trans-Africa biker types, bearded and tanned and wearing dark glasses. These strapping specimens make me realise that really I am too old for a trip like this and Gareth is too young. Put our ages together and divide by 2 and you get 31, still a bit old, but I think we compliment one another.

On that point it is so good to see how Gareth and I have settled into an easy familiarity with each other - something I so badly wanted at the start of the trip. Our silences are relaxed. We speak when we need to. I no longer worry about what Gareth thinks of me. I know, as I hope he knows, how I feel about him, although we have never said. It doesn't need saying. My pride and confidence in him as a person is total and complete. He is, in most ways, a young man now and I would find it almost impossible to reprimand him or tell him off or treat him like a child. He is his own man and I am proud of him. And despite my age and Gareth's youth, the other riders have accepted us as part of them so that, after a while, the age differences no longer matter.

And so, throughout the six-hour journey into more and more desolate desert, past wild camels and delicate dik dik who pick their way across the road as if on tip-toe, and the carcasses of animals dead from the drought, we seven riders came together and separated and came together again in that loose companionship of the road that we had heard so much about but have not experienced until today. The Germans are a small group within our group, Greg and Torbin loosely connected, having met twice before and spent some time together in Nairobi, Carl the Australian fallen by the wayside, and the two of us. We now belonged, although nothing was said. We passed through into Ethiopia together, found a guest house together, nothing formal, nothing planned, just a meeting of like minds with a similar love of motor bikes and adventure travel. I think we'll stay with them a while.

A brief comment on African border posts:

Bureaucracy, particularly the third world type, is like a game of poker played by travellers and petty officials who attempt to convince themselves and others that the charade that is played out in the scruffy little offices in the hot sun and dirt at borders really means anything. Stories of passports being examined with studious seriousness while upside down are all too real. Three, four and even five forms are filled in at various unmarked offices, each asking for exactly the same information and watched over by the same bored officials. And everyone knows that no one will ever read them or even compare the information on them.

Sometimes I deliberately fill in on the forms the first thing that comes into my head just to vary the monotony. Greg tells us he sometimes describes himself as "Brain Surgeon" or "Nuclear Scientist" on his forms opposite: Occupation.

Throughout the trip I used a fictitious address and phone number, playing the game with a calculated deference. Although, I must admit, that all officials we have encountered have been friendly and not once have we been solicited for a bribe.

Day 44

The change from Kenya to Ethiopia began about 400km from the northern Kenyan border as the rift valley vegetation faded to semi-desert and then the pure desert of Kaisut and Chalbi. Camels appeared staring contemptuously out of the bushes; English almost disappeared; the Muslim religion became prominent with Islamic verses in flowing Amharic script on the walls of small roadside shops; the features of the people became more Arab than negroid, both the men and women slight, spare of flesh, delicately boned. The women wear brightly-coloured loose clothing, almost like the Indian sari, covering the head but leaving the face clear, the skin light brown and beautiful so that, against the arid and dusty landscape, the women move, carrying water and fire wood, like bright jewels that do not cease to delight the eye. The sight reminds one of Biblical pictures of women at wells, a Madonna-like serenity of movement and facial expression. Men walk about hand-in-hand in unaffected, asexual familiarity, often with a teeth-cleaning stick in their mouths like a cigar or chewing bright green Khat leaves, a mild stimulant.

So far the people in Ethiopia seem very poor, many living in little huts made of bent branches covered with grass and, sadly, discarded plastic, so that they look from a distance like so many half tennis balls rather the worse for wear.

There are no bicycles at all anywhere near the southern border and very few cars. In the remoter regions, men can be seen carrying spears whilst others stand silently on the roadside with old bolt-action rifles across their shoulders. They carry the weapons with such dignity that, when seeing them, there is not the fear that a man further south with a weapon in his hands would instil. But that's a purely subjective opinion and might not bear any resemblance to fact. One simply *feels* safer here.

Today is a rest day, a wash and mend clothes and repair motor bikes day. It would be so easy to fall in with the timeless life-style of these young travellers who have no ties and no timetable, but we simply can't. In a way Gareth and I have approached their lifestyle and have valued every moment of the opportunity, but we (or rather I) do have ties and time does press on us. They are happy to spend 5-6 weeks, maybe two months in Ethiopia; we can really only spend 10-14 days. We are not on holiday; we are travelling from South Africa to Wales; my wife and daughter are waiting for us. I cannot act as if I am on holiday, as much as I would like to. It would be so easy to be drawn into their lifestyle, following the will-o'-the-wisp, chasing adventure around the next corner, the world your stamping ground, meeting and parting and meeting again in another part of the continent, sharing anecdotes and experiences, a loose camaraderie, pouring over maps, "I heard about..." someone says... "Watch out for...", "...they say you can get through by ship there... or maybe there... put the bike on a truck..." and the talk goes on like whispers of mist in the dawn. So, we will probably travel with the group tomorrow and then face reality and press on to Addis Ababa on our own as they take their more leisurely way.

Later in the afternoon, dirty and tired, three young Dutch and Israeli women arrived on a truck. They too have joined us, fellow travellers, and we share experiences together.

I will try to sleep this afternoon. I am not sleeping well at all - stifling heat and the drone of mosquitoes, constant noise from the ubiquitous and tyrannical radio, played loud enough to distort the speakers, wailing out a repetitive beat which gets into the bones. My nights are hell.

Day 45

The Ethiopian people we have met so far have been delightfully friendly and open and seem not to suffer from the begging habit one sees so often further south, despite being desperately poor. Gareth and I have just returned to our rooms in a most pleasant guest house in Yabelo, 250km into Ethiopia, after walking about the town.

A rather disconcerting trait of the Ethiopian children and even some adults is to shout out, the moment they see you on the street, a loud and peremptory "YOU!" (A variation of this is a rapid repetitive calling "YOUYOUYOUYOUYOU!") At first a little affronted at the seeming rudeness, our feelings were soon disarmed by the delightfully open, friendly smiles that were beamed upon us when we responded. It was engaging and special, if a little trying on the nerves, especially the loud "YOU's"! Often a child would stand close and take your hand in the street. This was a pleasant variation to the, "Hey, my friend - " with which we were greeted throughout Malawi and Tanzania and which usually was the opening gambit in an attempt to remove some of our money. I bought sweets and handed them out to a crowd of children who then followed us through the town, laughing and shouting, like Hamlen children.

The town's dusty streets are lined with typical small shops and Guest Houses and restaurants, the streets themselves clogged with goats which seem to have right of way into houses and shops and which eat anything they can find. It was lunch time when we first arrived here and we had a huge meal of some meat which wasn't beef or lamb or pork or chicken so I thought it wiser not to ask. Afterwards we had a cup of sweet black tea. We left a message with the owner to direct the other bikers, if he saw them, to our Guest House when they arrived, which he did.

An interesting observation we made about the Ethiopians is that, although the people and country are poorer than their countrymen further south, the society seems to work better. The guest houses are cleaner, running water that runs, electricity that works, food that is piquant, roads in very good repair and a functioning telephone system. Our guest house has neat beds of daisies and bougainvillea in the front and, in a corner, a grape vine growing over a trellis; a deep cistern stores water underground and a roof tank gravity-feeds the showers. In the south, very little seems to work: *"It is brokken..."*

Later: Over supper with the Germans and Torbin the Dane, we discussed our travels and where we hoped to go. Gareth and I have decided to do our best to get into Sudan - probably by ship to Port Sudan from Eritrea, then ride to Khartoum and try to get a truck into Lybia because of the soft sand. This is the desire of our hearts. If that fails then at least we will have experienced northern Sudan; at least we will have tried. If our carnets were validated for the Middle East, then we could try the route via

Saudi Arabia, Jordan, Israel, Greece, Italy and home or even Greece and overland via Eastern Europe. We just know we are not ready to give up and ship from Eritrea to Italy; that does not fit in with the spirit of the trip.

Afterwards Gareth and I walked back to the guest house through the dark flickering streets, smelling the strange warm smells of Africa, the lamp light glowing in the little street shops, inside yellow and cosy and muttering with life. Above, a million stars so bright and so tangible one could almost touch them. The night air was cool and I am completely well again; I looked up and thanked God, as I have done so many times before, for this incredible experience He has allowed us.

Day 46

Another side of Ethiopia was revealed today as we rode 330km north towards Addis. The weather was still delightfully cool and we followed a narrow tar road of indifferent but acceptable quality through a red land thick with thorn bushes which encroached on the road. Save for a few camels and isolated people, it was almost a deserted land: no cars, no trucks, no bicycles on the road and miles of semi-desert landscape broken by hills. Then we climbed higher to 3500m, the thorn trees gave way to eucalyptus which were imported in the early days for firewood and are now taking over; the camels disappeared in favour of goats, and people and vehicles clogged the roads. We passed fields of a bright yellow crop I hadn't come across before. In one field, a man was threshing in the ancient way by driving oxen over a pile of harvested grain. It was such an evocative scene that I stopped to take a photograph and learned that the crop is called *teff.*

Later, as we rode into more populated areas again, it became dirty. Passing a truck filled to bursting with humanity, a man spat on me. I felt violated, not so much by his spit, but by the intention behind it, like a slap in the face, a deliberate undeserved insult. I could not help reflecting on what I had done to deserve it - my white skin perhaps, the fact that I was more wealthy? I didn't know. I rather stupidly pulled in front of the truck and remonstrated with the spitter by standing on my foot-pegs, shouting and waving my arm about, making rude gestures. It was unnecessary and could easily have had me off but at the time it satisfied my soul.

It was a long but great day's riding and I felt again the loveliness of the road - that special feeling that, I believe, only travellers in remote parts of the world who have struggled to get where they are, who have the excitement of unknown adventure just around the next corner can truly feel. But, despite this, as so often before, something within is urging me to press on and on to home, suggest to Gareth that we ride all day and reach Addis early tomorrow morning, save a day. But then tomorrow is Saturday anyway so no visas can be obtained...

Finally we stopped at 3:30pm at the town of Shashemene. No water so no shower. After a rest and a read, we walked up the main street into the bustle and the noise and the dust, horse carts, wheel barrows, beggars, trucks and taxis, video and music shops and bars and shoe-shine boys and peanut vendors and booths selling everything, piles of second-hand tyres showing their canvas, and goats. Always goats. In the branches of a dead tree overhanging the main street, about fifteen Egyptian vultures roosted and, as we walked by, a man crouched and defecated in a storm water drain just off the main street...

Day 47

Fifty kilometres out of Shashemene, we passed lake Langano. A dirt road led towards it but we rode on. I thought of exploring it, decided against it and then, after about a kilometre, stopped Gareth and suggested we turn back. As it was we would have reached Addis by 1:30pm and, being Saturday, could really do nothing until Monday. So we rode back. And there, alongside the lake and parked next to a massive 6X6wd MAN truck (complete with micro-lite and off-road bike carried in the back) was Greg and his BMW! He was having breakfast with Brigitte and Stephen, two Germans cycling from Tunis to Cape Town, and, after coffee, Gareth suggested we stay here until tomorrow instead of pressing on to Addis. So we set up our tent, swam in the surprisingly cold lake, played boule with the German truck driver and his Ethiopian lover, lazed in the shade reading and generally living the good life! I had to keep on telling myself it was Saturday because part of me wanted to be on the road, putting distance NORTH under the tyres.

The driver of the MAN truck, Lothar, mid 30's, is also hoping to go through Sudan to Libya, also wanting to keep well clear of Egypt, but he, like us, will need a Libyan visa. His solution: "If I can't get one in Addis, I'll just fly back to Germany and get one there..." Money can do many things but, hopefully, perseverance, innovation and perhaps a little deviousness will do it too (I hope).

It's amazing what we are learning from fellow travellers we meet along the road about getting round in this world: fill in any vaccination you haven't got on your vaccination card and sign it yourself; if possible, have a stamp made and give yourself a visa; and, now that I have located Greg, (his suggestion) get hold of a photocopier and some cardboard of the right colour and make a complete set of carnets using his as a template with our details.

We shall see. Lothar says you can buy carnets for any country in the world from a guy in Germany who forges them...

Day 48

Spent a pleasant evening last night with the German cyclists and Greg eating soup and drinking strong black coffee (which Gareth calls "wake-up juice"), solving the problems of the world.

This Ethiopian coffee (called Boona), served black and sweet in small handleless cups, is the most delicious I have ever tasted. The Ethiopians themselves claim that coffee was first introduced to the world from their country and are rightly proud of it. The drinking of it is sometimes elevated to the realms of ritual, a process which takes about an hour and involves grinding the roasted beans and brewing the coffee over a slow charcoal fire, the room hazy with pungent incense, the mud floor of the hut covered with aromatic leaves and straw. But we have been warned that in tourist areas the unsuspecting are lured down narrow back streets with the offer of participating in a coffee-making ceremony and then robbed.

The 220km to Addis were completed without incident on a blustery day, the wind whipping up dust and hazing the distance. The road was flat, bumpy and pot-holed, the pedestrians and animals and trucks and taxi drivers suicidal, as usual.

Addis is a sprawling town set amongst hills and, after numerous enquiries (roads are not named in Addis) we found the Bel Air Hotel, haunt of trans-Africa travellers. Sphagetti for lunch in the Encounter Overland "garden" where we met Yo Yo, the Encounter Overland driver, a Frenchman, who sports a T-shirt with copulating red devils on the front. While we were eating, Greg arrived on his BMW and, about twenty minutes later, Lothar in the MAN truck.

We are all going to a Bob Marley remembrance concert in town this afternoon.

Day 49

The Bob Marley concert (with four of his children billed as special attractions) was typically and predictably a farce. We travelled into town in a rickety taxi of Russian make; the driver negotiated his way through heavy traffic, one hand on the hooter which he applied with abandon, the other swinging the steering wheel wildly from side to side - we realised why: there was a half-turn of play on the steering wheel. The car roof was in the process of separating itself from the body and we watched with alarm as cracks in the pillars widened and closed as we swerved around corners or to escape imminent head-on collisions with other equally mad, suicidal taxi drivers who were also using the "Who Dares Wins" philosophy of African driving. At the "stadium" there was a great deal of noise, a few thousand people, Rasta flags and enthusiastic calls for peace, love and brotherhood. Oh, yes, there was some execrable music too. Of course, none of the Marley family arrived. Greg suggested the organisers had been smoking too much dagga and forgot to invite them...

This morning after a cup of ginger tea, Gareth and I hired a taxi and set off for the Sudanese Embassy. It was closed off by a sheet-metal gate, but as we arrived a small door opened and we were ushered inside and led to a tatty gate house. Here, instead of signing a book and proceeding to the embassy, we filled in badly photocopied forms, left two photos and were told all should be well in 2-3 days - they just needed to fax Khartoum. Why a fax should take 2-3 days and why we filled in the forms in the gate house I did not enquire, but that is Africa.

Next, the Libyan Embassy. Again we were met at a sheet metal gate.

"Wait, I will ask," the gate keeper responded to my query concerning a visa.

Ten minutes later: "The Libyan consul is away at a meeting. You can come back in twenty days..." (I joke not!)

Needless to say, I argued for a long time, not losing my temper, requested permission to speak to someone face to face (he offered a telephone number) but to no avail. All diplomatic activity at the Libyan Embassy has ceased for twenty days because the consul is away at a meeting and I am not allowed to speak in person with anyone. Again, this is Africa...

And so, it is another two-day wait. I find myself getting increasingly frustrated at the delays. I just want to be on the road, making progress, and yet every day's travel seems to be hindered by bureaucratic delay. Our way seems clear into Sudan, but there is no guarantee that we'll get through to Libya. This kind of uncertainty is most frustrating because, if we are blocked at the Sudanese border, we will have to return to Ethiopia and try again elsewhere, with equally no guarantee of success. As it is, we can't get into Sudan from Eritrea, but have to back track to Ethiopia and enter via Gondar, the only border crossing open. But this will necessitate a re-entry visa into Ethiopia. Furthermore, Lothar is planning to go the same route as us in the MAN truck, but his timetable is much more relaxed so will be even slower. I would love to travel the Sudan/Libya route with him, but feel that he will be taking too much time. We need to get on.

WEEK 8

Day 50: Tuesday 4 March 1997

This morning we headed south for 90km, following a small road inland which led to a village at the foot of Mt Zukwala, an extinct volcano 3700m high. We were directed to a track which wound and zig-zagged steeply for 10km right to the top where there is a functioning Coptic mission complete with large round church and dormitories for 400 monks. Blissfully unaware, we visited the women's dormitory village overlooking the crater lake and were invited into a large room. Inside were mud ovens and stoves cooking *injera*, the sponge-rubber-like bread made in large thin discs the size of a tea tray, made from fermented teff. Not a word of English was spoken, but we were invited to sit and offered injera and delightfully cool water. Old women watched us with shy smiles through the smoke which hazed the room, high-ceilinged and unfurnished except for the raised mud platform around one side on which we were sitting, the hard clay softened by a folded goat skin. In one corner was a pile of cooked rounds of injera at least a foot high.

I asked permission to take a photo but was politely refused. Attempting to take photographs of scenes like this always makes me feel like a brash tourist boorishly intruding on personal lives, but photos *are* an important reminder of the beauty of one's experiences and, although I always try to get permission for a personal photo, even if granted there is always a sense of intrusion.

Once outside, an old man met us and led us down to the lake. He informed us he was a Christian, pointing to the Coptic cross around his neck. One's religion here is very much something to be declared, people often opening a conversation by declaring themselves Christian or Moslem, and inside homes and shops will be scripts from the Koran painted on walls or gaudy pictures of Jesus or Mary or St George slaying a plump dragon which lies on its back and seems to beg for mercy.

The crater lake was clear, blue and tranquil and surrounded by large pine trees. Standing in the silence of the bowl it was difficult to imagine that thousands of feet below on every side the land stretches away to the horizon, flat and yellow, the ground stubbled with the remains of the teff harvest, large yellow hay stacks like loaves of bread outside each small habitation and cows with their muzzles tied, threshing the pinhead-size grain from the straw.

Close to the lake a thick mat of grass floated on the water which undulated as we walked on it. I so wanted to swim in that clear pure water so high up this amazing volcano but the floating bed of matted reeds kept us from the very edge and I didn't like the thought of falling through. From the surrounding trees the hoarse choking sound of a bird echoed like the cough of a baboon. It was so beautiful, we were reluctant to leave.

We free-wheeled down the mountain because Gareth was low on fuel. From a village at the bottom came the *put-put* sound of a stationery engine which, on Gareth's insistence, we managed to locate. It was in a shed milling a mixture of grains brought in small sacks by women, the miller pale with dust in the shadowy room. The engine was Polish and Gareth inspected it with his usual interest.

Then back to Addis where I phoned the Sudanese Embassy. "No reply yet, maybe tomorrow ... or the next day..."

And so, once again, we wait.

Day 51

Another day of leaden frustration. The morning was spent marking time until the dreaded phone call to the Sudan Embassy at noon. Gareth, plagued by flies, repaired a puncture in the sun outside our room and checked the bikes over while I cashed travellers cheques and posted letters.

Later Gareth and I helped Yo Yo fit the gearbox to the Adventure Overland Bedford, and then it was time.

I dial with trembling fingers. The answer is so important and without it we are stuck. A disembodied voice says: "No, the fax hasn't arrived from Khartoum. No, I don't know when it will come. Please phone tomorrow."

If I only knew it would take a week or ten days or whatever, we could at least tour the north of Ethiopia and then return for the visa. But we don't know. This must come close to being in Hell for a normally active and decisive person to have his life and future dependent on some peasant of a clerk in a far-off benighted city too idle or inefficient to reply to a fax in under 4 days.

Obviously I have masochistic tendencies, because I phoned the Libyan Embassy. Perhaps, just perhaps, if I could get the Libyan visa, the wait will have been worthwhile...

Another disembodied voice on the phone: "...Why didn't you get the visa in South Africa?"

I explain.

"Please wait."

I wait. Then: "Why don't you get the visa in Khartoum?"

I explain. I could mention *Catch 22* but decide not to bother.

"Please wait."

"No, we don't give visas - only to residents. You must get it in Khartoum."

"But what if they too only give visas to residents?"

"Please wait."

"No. You must get it in Khartoum. Or from Tunisia."

"But we would have to *fly* to Tunisia; we are *here*, in Ethiopia! Why can't you give us a visa here? Isn't that what embassies are for - to issue visas?" (Rising hysteria.)

"Yes, but even if we give you a visa, it will take three weeks to a month to get permission from Libya..."

Aaaaaah!

We might have to go to Eritrea and see what we can sort out there. Before we left, a friend of Gareth's at school told him his father works in Eritrea and gave us his telephone number "just in case..." I tried to phone him - Dick Sanders - but all I could get was a recorded message.

Feeling very frustrated and with unkind thoughts towards all things African, Gareth and I took a minibus taxi to the Markato, a sprawling expanse of thousands of small shops selling everything to everyone. The taxi was cheap but you get what you pay for. Long delays in the hot sun while the tout called for passengers. When the vehicle was full, we pulled out into the street, thrusting other vehicles and pedestrians out of the way (may the most determined and with the loudest hooter win). After many such pauses waiting cramped and stuffy in the hot sun, we disgorged from the vehicle to be set upon immediately by beggars, touts, deformed people - the detritus of the city, offering, asking, begging, demanding, pleading, tugging the arm, the shirt sleeve, tagging along murmuring sotto voce, offering services, wares, advice, asking questions, staring; being whistled at and called "YOU!" "My friend" and "My brother" while one tries with only limited success to blot the whole cacophony out, not by any means catch someone's eye because that immediately solicits attention...

We desperately needed a replacement pump, ours having given up the ghost when Gareth tried it after repairing his puncture. Tackling the next stage of the trip without a pump would be asking for trouble so we asked and walked and asked and walked. The general philosophy at the Markato seems to be: If you haven't got, direct the person anywhere else regardless of the outcome as long as it is away from your shop.

We located the place at last but, of course, it was shut. The owner will be here at two, our self-appointed tout told us. So we waited half an hour in the sun, being crawled on by flies, stared at, questioned and solicited ad nauseam. At 2:00pm "...he will come at 2:30pm..." and at 2:30pm "...he will definitely be here by three...". Eventually he arrived and tried (as usual) to cheat me by asking double the price, a thin, smooth, dark-skinned young Indian man with protuberant black eyes. I called him a cheat (which relieved some of my tension), took the pump, paid the tout (who was aggrieved at the amount because, after all, he had waited two hours with us, determined to get his money), flagged down a taxi while fighting off the tout and sundry beggars and headed back to the hotel.

Bought oranges, a paw paw for tomorrow's breakfast, tomatoes and onions for supper with spaghetti, and a pineapple for dessert. Back at the Bel Air, Lothar was fitting $1000 tyres to his 6WD which he had purchased for $250 each. The scam works like this: a truck driver with new tyres stops at a roadside tyre shop, sells his tyres, replaces them with old ones and tells the owner that the new ones were ruined on the trip. The roadside tyre shop then sells the new stolen tyres at a quarter the cost of new ones. Truck drivers do the same with diesel and along the side of any road, youngsters stand offering litre bottles of diesel for sale.

And so I write this lying on my bed, flapping flies and thinking bad things about Africa. I so desperately long to be on the road, riding through the countryside, far far from people and on my way home...

Day 52

"Nothing yet," came the bored voice of Mohammed from the Sudan Embassy at noon. "Phone again tomorrow -"

My fervent prayers have not been answered and I want to scream and lash out at someone or something. After a brief wait I phoned the embassy again and pleaded with the telephonist for advice. She was helpful and understanding, said she would speak to the supervisor and phone me back. It is now 2.30 and she still hasn't phoned.

And so we read and chat with Greg and Yo Yo and tinker with the bikes. Gareth and I rode into the piazza and explored its multitude of shops this morning, drinking a cup of sweet tea served with a doughnut which was rather pleasant. More interesting than the thousands of shops is the life that goes on beyond and behind them, a life of which one is permitted the most tantalizing glimpses through narrow doorways opening onto steep and cramped alleys which wind between a rabbit-warren of shacks, corrugated-iron roofed, walls made of unpainted stone or mud, some two stories high with wooden balconies, the homes of the two million inhabitants of Addis, the shopkeepers and the touts, the taxi drivers and the beggars and the cripples, the men who sit on low walls and watch the cars, the children who converge on passers by and shout *"You! You!"*, the women selling oranges and pawpaws and tomatoes in their little piles on the side of the road, the owners of the goats and donkeys which roam the streets as if it is their natural habitat, which I suppose it is. The whole process of living and breeding and putting food in mouths is restricted to a façade of shops which line the streets, and we rarely if ever get to experience the loves and joys and tragedies that go on in the crowded shacks which clog the alleys behind. And I suppose it is self-centred of me in the light of such poverty and misery to be so concerned about my own frustrations but, selfishly, thinking of their tragedy doesn't lessen my own problems one jot.

Lunched at a local cafe with Greg, ordering three different Ethiopian dishes and sharing from the plates like the locals, tearing off bits of injera and scooping the spicy piles of *wat* into our mouths with the right hand, drinking freshly-squeezed orange juice and then finishing with coffee. We got to talking about travel and I reflected on my good fortune in experiencing this once-in-a-lifetime opportunity at my age and with a dependent family, to which Gareth said, "Once in a lifetime for *you!*" and I was happy. I think that somewhere in that phlegmatic head of his is the gleam of desire to travel on his own. If it happens and, as a result, changes the course of his life, my parenting will have done something positive.

To travel is formative, especially this kind of travel. It produces independence and strength; requires fortitude and ingenuity and an ability to live with yourself alone. And that sort of experience can seldom be bad...

The lady from the embassy hasn't returned my call and I can't call her because the telephone at the hotel is locked and the man with the key is out. All things seem to be conspiring against me...

LATER: The bikes are packed and ready to go first thing tomorrow. There is an excitement in me again and, if I could, I would head off now into the darkness. At last there is some sense of direction in our lives.

I finally got hold of the Charge d'affaires from the Sudan Embassy who assured me he would send a telex to Khartoum to expedite matters, but since they didn't work on Fridays it would only be acted on by Saturday and, anyway, sometimes it took two weeks for a visa to be granted. So Gareth and I have decided to do a 1400km loop of northern Ethiopia which should take 5-6 days, taking in Lake Tana and the Blue Nile falls and the rock-hewn churches of Lalibela and then back to Addis. Hopefully, by then, the visas will be ready and we can retrace the 450km to Gondar and then west into Sudan. Hopefully, too, the border will still be open - it is the only border that still is.

To celebrate, Greg, Alan and Paul (two Englishmen travelling by bus) Gareth and I ate out at a small restaurant in the piazza. Delicious pizza and red wine. Riding back in the dark, my lights blew because of the faulty regulator, I missed a corner, mounted the kerb and slid to a halt at the feet of a policeman astride his BMW. He was totally unfazed.

"Lights -" I explained, lamely.

He was quite happy to allow me to follow Gareth back to the hotel without lights.

Africa is a very relaxed place...

Day 53

Four hundred kilometres today, 10 hours (with puncture) and although the going was good, it is too much. I am very tired indeed. We must try to keep to a maximum of 300km per day on these roads. But it was so good to be on the move again even if it is only a large loop back to Addis. If we had our Sudanese visas tucked away in my pouch I would be feeling a great deal happier because still the spectre of refusal and further delay hangs over our return. Just two borders and we would be across Africa and at the Mediterranean. So frustratingly close, and the alternative seems to be a bureaucratic nightmare. I do so pray it will work out.

This morning we got away at 7:45am and fought our way for ten kilometres through an endless stream of cars, buses, taxis and pedestrians. The suburbs of Addis seemed to go on forever and the taste of exhaust fumes was bitter in my throat. But then we cleared a small ridge and before us lay the countryside, pale yellow with harvested teff catching the early morning light, the land seeming flat but rising gently between round hills. As we climbed, the air grew colder and a strong wind began to blow from the east. After an hour and a half of steady climbing, there could be no doubt that we were in the highlands: the crisp air, grass short and spongy, rivers rocky and cold. The men wore cloaks (shammas) covering their upper bodies and heads in much the same way the Basotho drape a blanket over their torsos. Horses made their appearance and many houses were built of stone instead of gum poles and mud.

The road was good but bumpy tar and we climbed and fell, switch-backing through pass after pass, the mountains rising higher and higher around us, rounded and stony but with very few rocky cliffs. Having had no breakfast, Gareth and I stopped at about ten, ordered an omelette and got spaghetti with hot spicy wat which was delicious. While we were waiting, some young girls approached us selling lightly-roasted grain - a mixture of mainly wheat, but with three other grain types mixed together with a little salt. The girls were beautiful, their hair long and black, long dresses covering their bodies, their faces having that open peasant look captured by early painters. They held flat baskets of grain easily in the crook of one arm, with a natural grace and economy of movement. We bought some and they were delicious, nibbling the smoky-flavoured grains we kept in our pockets.

The road continued climbing until we were riding through cloud. Suddenly in front of us the mouth of a tunnel appeared and we rode through in the pitch dark, a rough dirt surface below and the hewn rock above - an eerie feeling. On the other side the land fell away thousands of feet to a village and we paused to absorb its beauty. The road and tunnel, as well as numerous beautiful arched bridges made of local stone, are relics from the Italian occupation. The road is most un-African and at times one almost expects to see olive trees and aqueducts.

At the bottom of this massive escarpment the air was still and hot, the vegetation verging on semi-desert, stony ground, stunted shrubs and acacia thorn trees. But it must have been very fertile because feeding on the stalks left after harvest were thousands of sleek-looking cows, their horns thick and wide like the Zebu cattle found in some parts of Africa.

The road followed a wide flood plain, the grass growing on it green and pleasing to the eye. Although only a small trickle of water was flowing, the sight during the rainy season must be awesome judging by the masses of rock carried down from the mountains and lying in a tangled mass over the flood plain hundreds of metres across.

We continued for hours, following the wide bed of the river between towering mountains. Camels appeared again as if to reinforce the desolation of the place, but it was starkly beautiful and the small villages and many cows and goats softened the rocky hill slopes and towering mountains.

As the afternoon wore on, we were subjected to a few incidents of stone throwing from teenage boys which is most unpleasant. Some of it is mischievous - throwing some leaves or a light piece of wood at the bikes as we pass, but others are malicious and one never knows the difference until the missile is thrown. One learns to watch for these boys (it is always boys) bending down on your approach, a certain glint in the eye and a making ready. The easiest way to foil the attempt is to swerve and ride straight at the felons and, as they leap for safety, all thought of their missiles are lost and you are long past before they collect themselves again. It can be dangerous, though.

At some stage during the morning, I noticed a group of boys on the side of the road. One was holding out a large branch laden with berries (which he was obviously attempting to sell) across my path. Assuming that he would pull them away as I passed, I continued straight on until, with a most unpleasant blow, the branch hit me in the face and twisted my rear-view mirror loose.

Very angry, I braked as hard as the loose road surface would allow, U-turned and looked for the culprit. All I could see was scattering boys, running for their lives up banks, into huts, over fields. I set off after the one I believed to be the culprit who was sprinting madly across what looked like a fairly level ploughed field. I could see he was laughing and obviously confident of out-running me. Manoeuvring the bike through a shallow ditch, I accelerated onto the field which, close up, I found to be deeply rutted with old plough furrows which had hardened like concrete. The heavily-laden bike bucked and bounced and rattled but, angry as I was, I gripped the handle bars, stood up on the pegs (desperately hoping I wouldn't come off!) and kept up my speed. Soon I began to catch him. He was running for all he was worth, glancing over his shoulder as I bounced after him. His smile faded and, as I closed on him, a look of terror came over his face. He was trapped in the middle of an open field, no tree, no river, no friendly huts, no steep bank to run up and escape me. I knew I had him! With my front wheel centimetres behind his flapping legs, engine revving, he gave up, swerved to one side and collapsed on the ground. I leapt off the bike, rushed up to him and, as I bent down to grab him, he turned upon me a face of such terror, jabbering incoherently and pointing towards the village.

Without understanding a word, I grasped his meaning: it wasn't him; it was one of the others who had run towards the village. He was just a spectator. And a feeling of deep sadness and shame came over me. I felt like a bully. Cursing my quick temper and my petty sense of self-righteousness, I let him go.

It was a while before I could turn and extricate my laden bike from the deep plough ruts of the field and get it back on the road.

During the early afternoon we stopped for a cool drink and I asked at the local 'hotel' for a toilet. The waiter, misunderstanding, tried to serve me food. Three young and beautiful prostitutes understood and laughed their pretty faces and white teeth at me but didn't interpret, so I had to make crude and unbecoming gestures in mime. Ah! Now he understood!

With the echoes of their laughter in my ears, I made my way to the back and squatted over the hole in the floor, grateful that they had provided a basket of torn up bits of paper, just for me. However, it was when I tried to make use of them that I realised that the basket was provided for *used* paper, not paper to be used and I had great difficulty in the semi-dark trying to find a few of the least used pieces. It's incidents like this that can scar one for life.

On emerging onto the street it was easy to find Gareth again: he was the one white head protruding from the middle of a hundred staring black ones!

Finally, with 40km to go, Gareth stopped with a flat tyre. And it took one and a half hours and three attempts to repair it, watched all the while, as usual, by a crowd of locals who must find these mad strangers so very interesting; but when you have repaired a puncture, holed the tube replacing it, repaired the new hole to find that the patch didn't take and repaired it again, the silent stares and unintelligible comments and sniggers work somewhat on the nerves.

Finally we were away again and, as the sun was setting, casting long shadows down the valleys and turning the mountainsides pink, we climbed up from the valley floor that we'd been following for the past four hours, switch-backing up the side of the mountain with breathtaking views which I was, unfortunately, rather too exhausted to fully appreciate. Then over the top and, ahead of us, nestled in a shadowy valley like a Swiss mountain village (except the roofs are all corrugated iron) was the town of Dese.

I write this in a clean but expensive room while I wait for the geyser to heat water for a shower. Outside are the muted sounds of the street and later, when we are clean, we will look for something to eat.

Day 54

We are at the quaint mountain village of Lalibela, tired after an eight hour ride over rough roads, but clean and refreshed from a cold shower. The road today continued following wide flood plains with purple mountains, craggy now, high on both sides so that you wondered where the road could go to mount them. At intervals we passed a number of intact but abandoned tanks on the side of the road, their barrels pointing into the vastness of the surrounding mountains, mute testimony to the furious battles waged in these mountains between the Eritrean and Ethiopian forces over a period of thirty years.

As we have penetrated deeper into these mountains, the people have changed, the men's hair worn long, their shammas changing colour from village to village; sometimes the predominant colour will be a deep purple, sometimes an off-white or a dark green and, as you approach a village, patterns of moving colour, exactly the same shade, catch the eye before they metamorphasize into individual people. Today, Saturday, is market day and in the village squares thousands of people gather around stalls while donkeys and camels and people throng the roads. Gareth didn't want to stop and walk into the crowd but, in retrospect, he was probably wise because particularly the children react to passing strangers or, rather, white strangers, with what sometimes verges on hysteria, dancing and screaming and clustering around, touching the bikes, pulling on one's arms and jacket, asking questions.

The women here carry water in large earthenware pots, mostly round with two heavy, moulded handles and a spout, but some are narrower and look very much like amphorae. They pass a cord through the two handles and hold this across their shoulders whilst resting the base of the pot in the curve between the small of their backs and their buttocks. Some of the larger pots must carry 30 litres or more. The men, of course, don't carry water, but each man has his *dullah* or light stick, about one and three quarters of a metre long, quite unlike the heavy Zulu fighting stick or the knob-kerrie. Its function is more ornamental than functional and the men hold it always at the extreme end of the thicker side, often resting the length across the shoulders and draping the free arm across it in a casual pose. It reminds me somehow of the military swagger stick and perhaps serves much the same purpose.

As we progressed, the road deteriorated until it was all dirt and again riding was a strain because the loose stones on the surface sometimes felt like riding over ball bearings sprinkled on glass.

The road headed straight for one of the mountain sides and this time, instead of following the river valley, it climbed up and over, an awe-inspiring sight. Then came the turn-off to Lalibela, the road became narrow and rocky, snaking between mountain valleys. There were times when I felt we could have been in Lesotho, especially when it started to rain.

At 3:00pm we were forced to stop for another puncture - my bike this time but having learned the knack now, we repaired it first time and were off again in 40 minutes.

Lalibela is a small village perched high in the mountains. A pretty place, the houses so very different from the central African huts, many of them two stories high with wooden balconies and rusted corrugated iron roofs. Despite their height, the walls are still made from mud reinforced with gum poles.

The two Englishmen, David and Allen, whom we last met in Addis, are here having come up by bus so we ate supper together - injera and spaghetti with the usual very hot sauce. Then eight young people studying to become civil servants with the new European Commission in Brussels came in: English, Belgian and Portuguese, so the 12 of us had a most pleasant meal together, ending up with sweet black coffee, the beans for which had been roasted and crushed in front of us over a small charcoal burner.

During the evening, an English girl made an interesting comment: hearing that Gareth and I were father and son, she implied without malice that after three and a half months together we would probably be sick of each other's company - you know, teenagers and their fathers... And it was strange to think that, to most people, that is the norm, that 17-year-olds tend to dislike their parents as a matter of course; and yet Gareth and I have settled into such an easy relationship that our age difference and our being father and son just doesn't come to mind (at least not for me). I do not feel myself as old and Gareth young; I do not think of myself as The Father, with all the baggage contained therein. We are simply two people of like mind doing something we both want to do and that, really, is how it has developed between us. I hope when the trip is over things will stay this way. I don't see why they shouldn't.

Now, outside, the rain is rattling on my corrugated iron roof; my wet clothes from the walk back are hanging from nails driven into the wall; above me, adequate light shines down from a bare bulb and I am about to read my book. Early start tomorrow to visit the churches.

Day 55

Berhan, our 17-year-old guide woke us at 6:00am; a most pleasant young fellow, he feels that Gareth, also 17, is so much taller because he has led an easier life. Throughout the trip a common question to Gareth is whether he is married! (I'm sure that has done his ego some good.)

The churches, some cut vertically downwards up to 13 metres into the mountain rock, some making partial use of existing caves and others semi-monoliths are, as I expected, structures of beauty and wonder, an 800-year-old testimony to the religious faith of the makers. There is something awe-inspiring in the conception of an ancient people beginning a task so immense some have said it would have needed in the region of 40,000 stone masons to have completed the task. One can only think of the pyramids as a vague parallel and, like the pyramids, scholars and historians and local legend have woven science, myth and speculation into an attempt to explain the near unexplainable.

According to tradition, (we were informed by a straight-faced Berhan) Lalibela was assisted by angels in the forming of the churches, of which there are eleven in the immediate vicinity of the town. Evidently he and the angels completed the churches in 24 hours. Others hint at the involvement of the knights Templar and still others speak of extraterrestrial assistance...

My reaction on looking at the churches, however, was mixed as I tried to come to terms with what I was witnessing. What is significant about Lalibela is that, unlike most other historical relics, the churches are still functioning as they have done for the past 800 years. It being Sunday, services were taking place in all but one church and, despite the fact that Gareth and I were dressed in our dirty motorcycling clothes, I felt very much the tourist intruding on something spiritual. Outside the churches, worshippers leaned against the walls praying quietly or crouched in the sun reading their Bibles aloud, while from inside came the haunting sound of worshippers singing with deep spiritual fervency, the sound similar to the singing in tongues of a charismatic church, an intensely private worship of God in communal song, united in harmony of sound and feeling.

We didn't intrude into any of the services, but our mere presence made me feel self-conscious and embarrassed. I dearly wished I could just be alone, creep into a corner of a church and become one with the people worshipping God, but I couldn't, and it made me sad. Our white skins and western clothes label us outsiders, Berhan continued with his patter despite the surrounding worshippers, old women followed us begging and, somehow, we had acquired the services of a 'shoe boy' who followed closely, arranged our removed shoes in neat rows at the doorway of each church and stood guard over them.

And so, I am ambivalent about Lalibela. As a tourist/traveller, I have been moved by what I have seen; others would be too. And yet, as more and more people come to the area (it is pretty inaccessible now, but an airfield and a new road are under construction) it will of necessity lose the special quality that it has and become just another sight for camera-toting tourists and not the centre of a centuries-old living faith. I have been impressed by how relatively untouched the local people are by the tourists and our dollars, but the changes are coming. Already children follow up their engaging "Meester, meester " (so much nicer than "You! You!") with "Give me one Birr". Who can blame them? But the transition to beggar and tout from the dignity of their present lifestyle is inevitable and sad.

At the end of the day, Berhan invited us to his home, an invitation that Gareth and I accepted. He lives with his family in the lower section of a two-story round hut built of stone cemented with mud, the roof of the one constructed out of rough mud-plastered logs serving as the floor of the dwelling above. The hut was about eight metres in diameter and divided into two: a larger living room with low platform around the walls covered with skins as seats and a smaller section, separated by a sheet hung on wire, for sleeping. The floor was straw-covered and a small charcoal burner filled the room with sweet smelling incense. We were served glasses of traditional, home-made beer by Berhan's mother, a slight woman with a pale, serene face, necklace and bracelet tattooed on her skin. The beer is slightly sour but refreshingly cool and only slightly intoxicating; then a large tray of injera was served as well. All this while a young woman with delicate features was preparing coffee, first by pounding the beans with a heavy metal cylinder in the small hollow of a log, then boiling the grounds over a fire in a delicately fashioned coffee pot made of clay. We were then served with two delicious cups each before making our way back to our rooms. An intimate and special time.

Day 56

A day of lethargy and sleep. Perhaps it is the altitude or the lack of food, but I don't think it is that. Perhaps it is a kind of despair because, although this is a part of our travels and beautiful in its own very special way, it is really only a hiatus, a 700km journey north followed merely by a 700km return, with the uncertainty of the visa awaiting us and the radio speaking of fighting in Sudan against Somalis, Eritreans, Kenyans and Ugandans. Even if the Gondar border is still open, will they grant a tourist visa into a war-torn country? And if they don't, where to next? Eritrea? And if Eritrea, where to then? - it is boxed in by Sudan, Egypt and the Red Sea. I feel like a painter who has painted himself into a corner, knows it but is forced to keep on painting.

This morning there is a crisis in the village: a large gold cross was stolen from one of the churches last night. Gareth said he heard shots fired during the night and an explosion - perhaps a grenade - and today everyone is running about with guns and having earnest meetings.

While we were walking into town this evening, a bakkie with a loud hailer passed us. An urchin informed us that it was a call to all citizens to meet for prayer for the stolen cross. Suddenly, without warning, the streets erupted into shouting and laughter. People began to run towards the village centre. The urchin informed us breathlessly, his face aglow, that the cross had been found! From every house streams of running people emerged, thronging the road. The scene was reminiscent of storybook pictures of Jesus' triumphal entry into Jerusalem, the dark skins of the people and their off-white shammas adding verisimilitude to the spectacle, and I expected at any minute to see the waving and laying down of palm branches. We were carried along by the crowd into the village square. People jostled in, scaling the walls, clambering on the back of the bakkie which was attempting to nudge its way through the mass of people into the village square. Others crouched in the branches of trees like Zacchaeus, their shammas clutched about them. I couldn't discover whether the cross alone had been discovered or whether the thief himself had been apprehended, and knew in some dark part of my heart that if he was produced and offered to that throng I would give little for his chances of emerging alive.

And then the anti-climax. It was a false rumour. Sad and dejected, the crowd dispersed and, as if to echo the mood, the rain came down wetly. We huddled with others under the inadequate branches of a tree and an old woman voided her throat and spat, just missing my foot. She glanced up at me and her eyes met mine apologetically.

Later the rain stopped but by then we were wet, the road sticky with black mud. We walked back to our rooms for the night.

An Ethiopian man plays a reed flute in the darkness outside my room. I have been praying about the route ahead and the haunting notes intrude softly into my consciousness...

WEEK 9

Day 57: Tuesday 11 March 1997

(10,000km. Half way!)

Despite only doing 265km, today has been a hard ten-hour slog. I suppose running down an old woman, just missing colliding with a police Land Rover and a two-hour battle with a puncture didn't help.

I write this by the light of a 40-watt bulb hanging from the ceiling of a blue-painted, wattle-and-daub hotel room. We are on the second floor so I hope the walls hold up until tomorrow. I have washed in a bucket of icy water and feel reasonably clean despite sharing the 'bathroom' with an unmentionable hole in the floor which passes as a loo. Gareth is not feeling well but, as usual, he does not complain.

We were off by 8:00am this morning and, after being thoroughly searched for the stolen cross on the outskirts of the village, managed to find a little-used road which took us for 80km through the mountains. It was on this stretch that an old woman ran in front of my bike while I was trying to manoeuvre my way past cows, goats and a group of women who partially blocked the road. Fortunately I was going slowly but, despite locking up the wheels, I hit her in the legs and down she went. She sprang up nimbly and turned on me, her face suffused with anger. I leaped off the bike, ran up to her and checked her legs: no bleeding and nothing broken, fortunately, so I apologised as sincerely as I could despite knowing that she understood me not at all, and gave her a hug. But what I really wanted to say was, *Why run in front of the bike, you silly old faggot?* (What would we have done if I had broken her leg or hurt her badly? We were deep into the mountains and very far from any form of civilization.)

By this time all the women were crowded about me, shouting and gesticulating, letting me know in universally understood terms that they thought me lower than a camel turd and, if they were able, they would lay hold of me and do me a serious injury.

Knowing there was nothing further I could do, and wanting to put as much distance between ourselves and them as soon as possible before their husbands/boyfriends/second cousins arrived carrying sticks and bolt-action rifles, I remounted and attempted to start the bike. Of course, the old bitch simply refused to start, letting me down when I needed her most. Seeing my intentions, the old crone grabbed hold of the handle bars to prevent me from beating a hasty retreat. A tug of war resulted, me all the while trying to get the damn engine started without dropping the heavily-loaded bike on the road. Suddenly I realised what the old woman was doing: she had my sleeping bag, attached to the front luggage rack by bungee cords, half out and was tugging at it madly, obviously intending to claim it as compensation. I snatched at her hands shouting, "No you don't!" but her fingers were well hooked in the bungees and she wasn't going to let go - that sleeping bag was hers by some universally accepted tribal rite, probably a sort of eye-for-an-eye thing.

Gareth during all this was sitting on his bike watching with a grin on his face, offering no assistance whatsoever in my time of need. (Why on earth did I bring him if it wasn't to leap to the aid of his poor ageing father when needed?) Fortunately we were on a slight downhill so I gave up trying to kick-start the bike (Quick comment: Firstly, where was the electric start when I *really* needed it? and, secondly, those who have attempted to kick-start a reluctant XT500 will have some idea what I was going through. Add to that a crowd of screaming, grabbing women and an old crone who had her claws into my sleeping bag and was attempting to drag it out or have me and the bike over, whichever came first - and you will understand what I was going through.) So, I leaped off the bike, ripped the old crone's hands free and, in a rather undignified fashion, push-started the bike. When I glanced back, all the women were picking up stones and throwing them at us. We were very fortunate that there were no men about because most of them carry guns; and what would have happened had I broken her leg or injured her seriously doesn't bear thinking about. A very lucky escape!

The police 4X4, very briefly, came rather rapidly around a blind corner of a very narrow, rocky mountain road. As we were both in the centre, we had to take very quick avoiding action; instinctively, I swerved to the left instead of the right and, with locked wheels and bulging eyes, the driver managed to stop within a metre of me. I quickly explained that we were from the UK and drove on the left, etc etc - an explanation he graciously accepted.

After the excitement, we climbed steadily into the mountains until we entered cloud and rode through semi-twilight with visibility about 20m. The area we passed through had experienced quite heavy rains and the road was glutinous with clinging mud which threatened to have me down several times. Then, finally, we emerged from the clouds and followed the track down a beautiful pass with range upon range of mountains disappearing into the purple distance on all sides, wide cultivated valleys between and a sense of endless space.

Reaching the plains and human habitation again, we had just decided to stop for a late brunch when Gareth discovered a flat back tyre. Within moments we were surrounded by a crowd five-deep. Pumping didn't help, so Gareth started his bike and walked it back to a nearby 'hotel' while I tried to retrieve one of his gloves which had dropped and been quickly taken by someone in the crowd. Their gawking and laughter and sullen silence when I asked for the glove annoyed me more than a little so, when some teenager demanded money, I confess I said a bad word to him. Seeing my anger and contempt, the one who had picked up Gareth's glove ungraciously returned it to me.

We ordered egg and bread and coffee and then started on the tyre. It took us two frustrating hours and four attempts before we had the job done. The reason this time was that the hole, for some reason, was on the *inside* of the tube where it fits into the wheel rim. Usually, as you pump up a tube, pressure against the tyre keeps the patch firmly in place; on the inside where the tube fits into the rim depression, there is an air gap there until the tube is quite well inflated. Lacking the tyre to press against, the patch repeatedly blew off before it could be held against the rim by its own inflation. A most frustrating time.

The afternoon ride of 120km was long and tiring and I felt a sad heaviness upon me. I think it is knowing that we are heading south, back-tracking to Addis; and home, wife and daughter are still very far away in the opposite direction and the way to them uncertain. I do so pray we will be able to get through to Sudan and then Libya...

Day 58

Gareth hit a cow *and* a goat today so, with his donkey of two days ago he gets 9 points. With my 10 points for the defenceless old lady I am still beating him.

The animals and humans in Ethiopia make riding more than a little trying. As with cars, trucks and buses, the philosophy seems to be: Get around the obstruction any way you can. Drivers of animals make little or no effort to get them off the road; people not only don't move off the road, but step into it without looking then leap back like startled hares as if shocked that there might be a vehicle trundling along behind them. And, of course, one can't not mention every child who finds it obligatory to scream, shout, throw a stone, pretend to throw a stone, roll a ball under the wheels, act as if he is about to commit suicide by leaping under the wheels or pushing his smaller friend to his immediate and gory death. Perhaps they have lessons in school: Maim a Motor-Cyclist with a Single Stone 101. Animals, unless given a very wide berth, tend to panic and run in any direction and, as Gareth has discovered, often under the wheels of the bike. All three: the cow, the donkey and the goat went sprawling ass over tit, but scrambled to their feet none the worse for wear (I hope) and, fortunately, Gareth managed not to spill.

Needless to say, we didn't stop to discuss possible compensation (like sleeping bags) with the owners.

We left Desse at 9:00am after changing money and a quick breakfast. And then it was 450km of long, hard riding until we reached Addis again at 6:30pm. No punctures today, thank goodness, but Gareth's bike seems to be falling apart again. Over the last 1000km one rear wheel adjuster snapped in half, one rear brake shoe disintegrated, his clutch cable snapped and he lost bolts from the exhaust flange and chain cover. Will try to sort it all out tomorrow while I visit a travel agent. I am going to explore the possibility of flying ourselves and the bikes to Tunisia from either Addis or Asmara - that is, if the Sudanese visas are not ready. We will see...

Day 59

First thing this morning, filled with trembling anticipation and fear, I phoned the Sudanese Embassy for one last time. "Good morning. I just wondered whether permission for our visas has arrived from Khartoum yet -?"

"No, nothing yet. Phone tomorrow -"

Enough. I give up!

So, while Gareth headed into Addis in a taxi to sort out the welding of his rear wheel adjuster, re-shoeing his brakes and getting another clutch cable, I rode into town to try sort out a ship or a flight around Egypt and Sudan. And I had a most depressing morning: no direct flights from Addis or Asmara; all routed via Egypt, the cost about $1600 ie almost all the money we have left. The shipping companies I visited referred me to Eritrea. In fact, everyone seemed to be only too eager to refer me to someone else, to pass the problem on, as it were, so that the work involved would be done by someone else in the African way.

So we have made the decision: tomorrow we head for Eritrea. Should take five to six days.

Interesting - and somewhat sobering - we met some Germans who are travelling in a Land Cruiser. They had friends who, in June last year, tried the Sudan-Libya route. They entered Sudan, were refused entry at the Libyan border and turned back, but Sudan wouldn't let them back in because they didn't have a multiple-entry visa. So they were stuck between the Libyan and Sudanese border posts in the desert for a month until the Libyans relented and allowed one of the party through to telephone Germany for help.

Day 60

Last night we had pizzas with Yidshack and Offer, two Israelis who are staying at the Bel Air. They have been robbed five times in Ethiopia and Kenya, two of the thefts classic and bare repeating. Camping at the Blue Nile Falls, their tent was slit open in the early hours of the morning with a blade so sharp that it penetrated the tent wall, back pack and some of the contents in one slice. $900 was stolen while they slept, oblivious of what was going on. The second: before boarding a bus, Yidshack was passing their two back-packs to Offer who was perched high up on the roof rack. After passing the first up, he bent down to pick up the second at is feet but it was no longer there. A fully-loaded back-pack had simply *disappeared* in the flicker of an eye, containing everything he possessed: clothes, passport, money, the lot. In the time it took for him to lift the first back-pack and bend down to pick up the second, it was *gone*. Two Englishmen and a Canadian woman, sharing the meal with us, had also been robbed - three times.

Evidently tourists/travellers especially are targeted, followed until we buy something and reveal the whereabouts of our carefully stashed money; thereafter follows a well-rehearsed set up: sometimes a group of children will stage a fight and blunder into you, or you will be approached with hand clasps and signs of affection or the more usual bump or group cluster. Gareth and I have been very lucky; careful, but also lucky because these people are experts and we, I think, are mere babes in the wood. We have, also, become complaisant; my neck purse and locked-and-double-tied fanny bag, neither of which leaves my person unless I am in bed, are probably child's play to these professionals. Greg had a most cunning wallet attached to his lower leg like an ankle holster and most other travellers use money belts and concealed pockets sewn into the lining of their clothes.

After faxing a letter to Wales, we were away by 9:00am, but it took us an hour to negotiate the 20km of suburbs, a maze of clogged roads with no names or sign posts. Unfortunately we took a wrong turn and headed 35km west before discovering our error and so, back to Addis, back into the chaos, and onto the right road. By this time it was almost 12:00 and we'd come an effective 15km away from the city centre. But once out of town we made good progress along very bumpy tar over flat rolling countryside, checkered with newly-ploughed fields, old harvested lands of wheat and teff, yellow in the clear sunlight, and pastures of very short yellow-green grass.

We stopped when tired for cool drinks or tea and coffee - black and very sweet - and at midday paused for a lunch of injera. Then, suddenly, the land fell away into the Blue Nile Gorge - Africa's Grand Canyon. The road snaked downward for 20km to the bottom, getting hotter and hotter as we descended. Sadly, the tar had broken up and not been replaced, so it was as if we were riding on dirt all the way to the bridge at the bottom.

On the way down we came across yet another crashed truck. It had been carrying a load of grain, had lost its brakes on the way down and turned over. The cargo - or what was left of it - was being guarded by a lone man who gratefully accepted some water. At the bottom of the valley without the cooling breeze from the bikes it was like standing in an oven. Then up the other side for 20km until we reached the pretty little town of Dejen where we found a clean walled 'hotel' with cold shower and small rooms with bed and table and green-painted walls. We unpacked, stripped off boots and drank a welcome cup of tea then rested. Even though we have only covered 310km, we rode with very few breaks for 8 hours - very tiring on the mind and body.

After supper, Gareth and I walked down the main street, capturing the distinctive mood of these truck-stop towns. The streets are cluttered with people, mainly men, who appear out of the darkness robed in white shammas like apparitions. Often we are greeted or people call to us from across the road, friendly calls. The atmosphere is balmy and festive with local music thumping and screeching from every open door; wafts of incense from the smoky interiors of houses, flickering with lamplight, perfume the air; goats wander across the road and children play in the street. Every second structure is a 'hotel', a bar or a coffee house, looking after the drivers of the large Fiat trucks and trailers that line the dusty sides of the road or bellow through with a blast of diesel fumes.

Near the outskirts of town we passed a little box of a shop and bought sweets. Two young lasses, about fifteen or so, took a shine to Gareth, got sweets off him and invited us into their tea shop. We complied amidst much giggling. The one sat herself next to Gareth, rather close so that her thigh rested against his, and gave him and me such brazen looks that I felt quite embarrassed. My suspicions were confirmed when she assured us in a husky whisper that she was "Clean". We drank tea while she told Gareth that he was "beautiful"(!), pulled the hair on his arms and showed him that hers were smooth, then poked a finger into a hole in his trouser leg, perhaps trying to get the message across by demonstration (Gareth being more than a little slow in these matters). Realising that she was going to get little of interest from him, she made admiring references to my beard, leaned close and mouthed something in my ear which I assume was a rather tempting price. I was flattered but not tempted.

We finished our tea and left.

They were both rather delightful, the less brazen one having a gentle beauty and a quiet manner that was most fetching. The experience made me feel quite young again!

Day 61

After saying goodbye to our young ladies from last night, we headed out of town onto a dirt road, fairly smooth but, as always with stony dirt, tiring to ride on because one's concentration has to be so much more intense. After 40km Gareth had yet another puncture - out of town, fortunately, so we only had 47 watchers and we did the job first try in 45 minutes. (We're becoming quite blasé about puncture repairs now.)

Our road led us over undulating land, patched with fields thronged with large herds of cattle. The small villages we passed through were pretty and, throughout the day, large trees dotted the land - gum, flat crowns and large dark-green figs. Again the land plunged into a gorge with the Blue Nile snaking its way along a hot valley, then up again into the cool air of the highlands. At four we reached the junction to the Blue Nile falls and, after 30km, arrived at a small village heavily-populated with donkeys (who seem to feel that their natural domain is the road), left the bikes in charge of a young guard (these chaps guard the bikes with the utmost dedication, with stick, stones and threats if need be) and walked the one and a half kilometres to the falls.

Not expecting much because of the lack of water in the river, we were pleasantly surprised at the beautiful sight of water cascading over rocks in a gorge about 300m long, the spray reaching us high on the opposite side. I chased the inevitable self-appointed guides away so we could sit in silence and solitude and absorb the scene and then, as it was getting late, we headed back into the setting sun to Bahir Dar where boys on bicycles led us full tilt through back streets to this 'hotel', clean and cosy, the bikes secure in the courtyard and a cool shower of rain rattling on the corrugated iron roof.

Day 62

The 180km to Gondar was along a rough, dusty road that ran through a flattish, rocky landscape, desolate and hot. We could only get doughnuts for breakfast and stale cakes for lunch and no coffee because the electricity seems to be off throughout the north. No petrol was to be obtained from any of the garages so we resorted to black market petrol siphoned from a drum at the back of some dingy shed at 50% more in price, as well as tipping the fellow who led us at a jog up the main street of the village with the rest of the population galloping behind in the chase. We then wait, surrounded by a dark mass of humanity, peering, touching, trying the clutch lever, the accelerator, some begging, others making comments so that all laugh. And then the questions:

How are you?

What is your name?

Are you a tourist?

What is your country?

Where are you going?

Can I have your address?

Give me a pen.

Is this your son?

Is he your first born?

Throughout Ethiopia, the questions are the same.

Then the one who assisted the one who directed us to the petrol wants money as does the one who carried the can, but I'm not that gullible any more. The disappointed ones, those whom we have not given money to, most offended, continue gesturing their services and holding out their hands until we ride away, the crowd scattering with expressions of real fear as we kick the bikes to life.

After Gondar, however, the road climbed steadily to over 3000m into the foothills of the Simian mountains. Immediately the atmosphere changed: the air became cooler, the people more friendly; children wave and smile instead of throwing things and behaving like imbeciles. The roads had been well constructed by Italian engineers during the occupation, but have since been sadly neglected. In places the original foundation shows through and often we were riding over what looked (and felt) like a cobble pavement. It reminded me of an old Roman road over the mountains.

{No diary for Mon 17th March, Day 63}

WEEK 10

Day 64: Tuesday 18 March 1997

Although we managed only 212km today, it took 8 hours of hard riding. The road was very rough but meandered through steep and beautiful passes through the Simian Mountains. If we were not climbing steeply up the side of one mountain, we were snaking our way down another, the tops cool and beautiful, a blue vista of range upon range of mountains disappearing into the distance; but in the valleys it was hot and breathless, everything covered with a fur of dust, the river beds almost dry and the few villages we passed through poor. But the mountain people are friendly and we stopped every now and then for cool drinks or tea or lunch and instead of crowds of staring insolent faces, we were joined by small groups of children who eyed us shyly and smiled when we looked at them. If children did become too forward or called us with the all too familiar "You! You!", the adults in the vicinity reprimanded them. A lovely change from the lowlands. Not that they didn't try to rip us off. A man selling black market petrol insisted for about 15 minutes that a two-litre jug actually contained three litres and only conceded the point with a sheepish smile when he realised I wasn't going to be taken in.

As we neared the end of our day's ride we came across more and more wrecks left on the sides of the road from the war with Eritrea - trucks, truck mounted AA guns, 88mm howitzers, tanks and armoured personnel carriers. In one place, near a small bridge, we stopped and explored a graveyard of about fifteen trucks and other vehicles, ripped apart by shells or bombs. The ground all about was littered with exploded and live AA shells from the burning trucks.

There must have been some fierce fighting along the passes and at the bridges in these mountains, and the destruction wreaked on the vehicles, the thickness of metal ripped apart and twisted, was a horrific testimony to the destruction of war, and left one with a strange sensation in the belly, knowing that what had been done so visibly to thick insentient metal, had ripped through the living flesh of human beings at the same time. A sobering thought, contemplating the futility of war and what man will do to man.

It is evening. I have showered in gloriously cold water and slept a little, my body exhausted from long days of riding over bad roads. At 7pm, as has become our custom, Gareth and I walked down the main street of town - a balmy night, alive with sounds and smells and people, mostly male. Little boys approach us quietly, offering bowls of roasted peanuts, flat baskets of various seeds, cigarettes and gum (sold by the packet or individually), scratch cards, teeth-cleaning sticks, boiled eggs and salt. We buy peanuts and eat them as we stroll. The taste is piquant and salty, so the mouth craves for more. A restaurant with blaring music serves us fried meat cut into small squares, bread and salad. We eat with our fingers. Then to a pastry shop where we select pastries by the light of a candle and sit on chairs under a canopy next to the street; we drink cups of strong black coffee, so sweet it is like syrup. The child street-sellers creep up close and watch us discretely, every now and then offering their wares with silent gestures in the hope of a sale or to excuse their closeness. I buy a teeth cleaning stick and give a Birr to a little boy with withered legs who walks on his hands...

Day 65

Completed the last 100km in Ethiopia by 1:30pm after spending a short time in Axum looking at the obelisks and a huge old Ruston Hornsby stationery engine. Gareth picks these things out from the general clutter in villages and barns and, I think, it's all he looks for. It's about the only thing that stimulates him into any form of enthusiasm - not even the sweet young thing touching his leg the other night excited him as much as this engine (and long may it last!)

It took us two hours to get through the borders after dealing with typical African bureaucracy. It turned out that, quite by chance, we had reached the Eritrean border on the last day before our visas expired. Very fortunate for us because we hadn't bothered to look at the expiry date. Had we arrived just one day later, to get through to Eritrea would have involved a hefty bribe or being told to return to Addis to renew the visa.

Then 10km of shocking tar road, climbing up a high escarpment. After that, the road improved and we sped along as if we were on a winding race track - exhilarating stuff for 80km, reaching Asmara at 5pm. Met with Dick Sanders - the father of one of Gareth's school mates - and his partner Jules, who are putting us up for a few days.

Will begin to search for a ship tomorrow.

Day 66

The morning was spent servicing the bikes - 12,000k service. I had the Jerry can welded up yet again and altered the rack that holds them. (As I originally designed it, the jerry cans hang on only one of their three handles to enable them to drop away in case of accident so that, hopefully, I wouldn't become toast in 40 litres of burning petrol if the whole lot caught fire while grinding away along the road in a trail of sparks. But the weight was cracking the handles so I extended the angle iron to support all three handles and spread the weight.)

After lunch Dick took us to a shipping agent who wasn't particularly helpful: ships will only take a complete container, he claimed, even if the bikes only fill it one eighth. Cost: $1400. To fly them $1300. This does not include Gareth or me.

But we will keep trying. Again the frustration of waiting. We can't explore Asmara because we have to wait by the phone in case Dick or the agent calls. In the house there is nothing to read, no radio or TV and the books we are carrying have all been read at least twice. If nothing comes up tomorrow we'll have to ride the 100km to the port of Massawa and talk to the agents there or even contact a ship's captain direct on the docks.

A certain amount of relief today in that we have got visas for Italy. Rather difficult, though, because they will only allow us 20 days and we had to say when we expected to be there - almost impossible with no idea when or whether we can get a ship. Tomorrow we leave for Massawa.

Questions about the way ahead crowd my mind and make me constantly on edge: How does one get aboard a ship with two motor cycles? The agents seem totally uncooperative and unconcerned. A repeat of Addis, in fact. "Maybe a ship in 3-4 days. Phone Monday -" (Echoes of the Sudanese Embassy.) "Only freight, no passengers. Must be in a container. Maybe in a crate." Priced air tickets for Gareth and me to Italy: $840 each, one way. Hope we can get on a ship with the bikes. And how on earth do we crate the bikes in Massawa?

Asmara is an interesting city - clean and orderly, the people polite, friendly and, strangely, very Italian. No beggars and no peremptory shouts of "You! You!" One can relax and let down one's guard when walking along the palm-lined main street with cafe chairs and tables on the sidewalk or, as we did this morning, make our way through the market into the old quarter where we explored a maze of little alleys, truck-lined, off-loading various grains and chilli and spices. Then into the 18th century where artisans sit in little booths fabricating things from scrap metal, turning truck springs into ploughs (it sounds almost Biblical!), wire into chains, 44 gal drums into buckets and injera cookers. There was every type of scrap iron, empty ammunition boxes, truck engine and body parts, old Primus stoves. Gareth was in his element. Yesterday we discovered an interesting stationery engine with a cluster of pipes going from the header to footer tank for cooling - something we've never seen before and today, in amongst the scrap, another which looked like a Petta. When asked the price, the first said 10,000 Birr and the other 5000 - R700 and R300 respectively. We laughed.

Lovely phone call from Glynis last night and expect another tonight, but, sadly, still no job. Still no conclusive information about my severance package so this adds to my feelings of guilt and pressure, not only about how to get us and the bikes to Wales, but also what job I am going to be able to get when we reach there.

Ah, well, at least Glyn was cheerful and said she had found a church so, as any husband knows, if your wife is happy, all will be well.

Day 68

Above me, high up against a dark wooden ceiling, an ancient fan rattles and squeaks, speeding up and slowing down, straining against worn, dry bearings. The room is hot and still and airless; outside on the wide verandah, men sleep away the hot hours from 12:00 till 4:00pm when work begins again until 7:00pm. We are in Massawa, with its bombed and shrapnel-riddled buildings and its causeways over pale clear water, a harbour with cranes and a few ships tantalisingly offering the possibility of passage out of here but closed off by a shut gate, a high fence and a surly guard who repeats mechanically, "It is not possible..."

We left immediately after breakfast, bidding Dick and Jules a sad farewell. They had been good to us, most helpful with their advice and support but, despite their local knowledge, they could not get us aboard a ship or help us fight our way through the stultifying wall of bureaucracy. The road to the coast wound down the escarpment, dropping 2000m in 50km, the temperature rising steadily as we dropped; vegetation greened and smelt musty and damp because relief rain against the escarpment gives these slopes the highest rainfall in Eritrea. Then onto the flats, a stifling heat and close to pure desert with a long low wedge of mountain following the coast; and camels and goats and the battered remains of tanks and army trucks pushed to the side of the road. Into the heavily bombed town with three tanks on pedestals to commemorate their recent victory against the Ethiopians.

We tried without success to get into the harbour, asked fruitlessly at the offices of clearing and forwarding agents and were finally directed to the ERSTAS shipping agent. It was Saturday, getting late in the afternoon and I desperately wanted some definite news to bide me over until Monday. I couldn't bare waiting until the offices opened in two days before getting some information that would give us hope of a way forward. We entered a dim office. Explained our problem to a pleasant-faced man at a desk who looked up in a book and said that, yes, it seemed that there was a ship arriving on the 28th, six days time, which called in at Italy and he pointed out another office for me to enquire. There, a brusquely rude man snapped that there were "no ships calling at Italy, go fill in forms at a forwarding agent, we can't help you". Back to the gentle-faced man; I told him of the rudeness of his colleague and that I was close to despair.

"Do not despair," he said kindly. "There are people who are like that. Come back on Monday because now it is late and we can do nothing until then. I will look after you personally."

His kindness brought me close to tears.

Because of the heat, Gareth and I retired here to our room and rested while the exhausted fan stirred the humid air above us. And I got to thinking of Glyn and Jem and home; and once again a deep sense of loneliness has come upon me, a sense of the importance of family and ones you love and a place to call "home" - these things are so much more important than all the adventure of travel and all the excitement of exotic lands. I am grateful that Gareth is with me and, although saddened that our trip has, in a way, failed, there is a tiny sense of peace and anticipation which comes over me: we're going home! And although Gareth and I have spoken of the possibility of travelling south from Italy to Tunisia and from there into Libya, riding as far south in Libya as we can get in an attempt at bridging the gap in Africa caused by the boat trip, north/south, joining as near as possible the lines of latitude, something in Glynis' voice last night as she said goodbye, and the words she used, have made me realise that the bright cheery tone she has adopted on our few phone calls before are a brave façade. I need to be home with her, supporting her through the trauma of an emigration and the setting up of a home; and any unnecessary delay or deviation from the route to her would be an act of selfishness despite my deep desire to go to Libya and complete the Africa crossing we had set our hearts on.

My conscience and my desire to fulfil our dream debate like good and bad angels inside my head...

We will see...

Later: Lying on my bed in the dim light of late afternoon, I happen to glance at an old wardrobe against the wall. Its door is fitted with a full length mirror, the backing patched and wrinkled with age. And I see myself reflected there, arms behind my head, eyes closed. And with a shock I realise that it is Gareth.

What an awesome responsibility it is to bring someone into the world who looks something like you, who bears outside (and inside too, in a way) the stamp of your own nature and yet, so clear in Gareth on this trip, his own person, an individual who is himself, capable of making decisions, feeling, thinking, responding to God or rejecting Him, relating to me and the world in his own unique way, and yet still having something deep down in the genes of me that he can never reject or deny.

And I realise just how precious he is to me and how empty life would be without him and what a terrible thing true loneliness must be.

Day 69

Sunday and a day of waiting. Got up late, bought cereal and fresh cold milk for breakfast then rode out along the dirt road towards Assab for 30km. A rough and corrugated road; I hope we don't have to do the full 650km to Assab to get a boat as some have suggested.

Stopped at a scrap yard of war debris, shattered tanks and trucks, rail coaches and containers. There is a macabre fascination in both of us about these things - the thought that people fought and died here, crouched in these vehicles, the violence of war all too palpable, leaving one, finally, with a sense of tragic waste. But while we were treading about in this detritus of war, I looked down and realised that we were bumbling about amongst live shells, grenades and other lethal things that had just been dumped there. Very gingerly we stepped our way out and back to the bikes - but not before Gareth pocketed a few live 50mm shells as souvenirs.

After lunch we headed out north for 8km to a beach where we swam in cool, clear water. With sudden realisation, Gareth looked at me and exclaimed, "We're swimming in the Red Sea!"

Hope and earnestly pray that tomorrow will yield positive information about a ship.

Day 70

We reported to the shipping office at 9:30am and all seems positive. Our ship, the Omo Wonz, will be docking in Massawa on Wednesday and, pending the captain's OK, the bikes will be crated and loaded for the Italian port of Livorno. The trip should take two weeks and there might be room for us as passengers. *Yes!*

More waiting.

WEEK 11

Day 71: Tuesday 25 March 1997

To help pass the time while we wait for the Omo Wonz to plod its way towards Massawa, we rode 80km back towards Asmara to try to find a winding track into the mountains we had seen on the way in but, as we climbed the escarpment, a heavy mist descended and we couldn't see anything, so we turned back. At a small village we stopped, wet and cold, and ate some disgusting goat soup, then followed a rocky camel track half way down a mountain for fun, but got cold feet and headed back - one needed to be a goat or a camel to negotiate the rocks! It was like riding up a stony river bed; Gareth fell twice and broke his rear view mirror. (Har!)

Hope the boat arrives tomorrow...

Day 72

It is late evening, Wednesday, and I have just seen, through the harbour fence, a tug nudging our ship into dock. At last, tangible evidence of the fact that we are on our way home! These days of waiting and uncertainty have been most unpleasant; at least when we are on the road, progress that we can see and feel is being made. Then I am in charge of my life, giving it direction, shortening the distance between me and my wife and daughter. But the waiting, the helplessness of one's life in the hands of someone else...

Came across Lothar - he of the 6WD MAN truck we first met in Ethiopia. He told Gareth his Sudan visa permission has come through and he will be travelling back to Addis to get it and then, as we had planned, through Sudan and into Libya. And immediately the disappointment, the "if only's" and the "what if's". I know Gareth was weighing up the options as I was: Is our visa there? Could we make it? Do we have enough time? Would the almost certain chance of delay be fair on Glyn?

If we were blocked in Sudan, then we would be forced back into Ethiopia (another visa), another visa for Eritrea, back to Addis, back to Asmara, right where we are now, waiting again for a ship (and the ships come only every two weeks. What if we just missed one?)

It was tempting, *so* tempting, but impractical. If I were younger and unattached and with unlimited time, I would jump at the chance...

I phoned the Sudanese Embassy, more to assure myself of the impossibility, but also, secretly, to keep all options open just a little longer. "Closed," they said, after I managed to get someone to translate. "Phone tomorrow..."

I'll take that as a closed door.

And then our ship sailed in. One door closes, another opens, the signs clear as to what route to take. But there is still such an ache in my heart. Perhaps if we can get to Libya from Italy, travel south into the desert, it will go away.

We will see...

Day 73

It's 9:00pm, the bikes are finally loaded (uncrated) onto the Omo Wonz after 13 hours of waiting and, intermittently, filling in forms. We feel quite lonely without them, as if a member of the family is missing. We still don't know whether we can get a passage on the ship; the captain, a large man from Ghana, most approachable and friendly, is happy to take us; our agent is also most helpful and friendly and is happy for him to take us, but the rude one in the ERSTAS office bluntly and angrily insisted, "No passengers!"

I will try the manager tomorrow without putting too much pressure. If he refuses, we might have to fly; a costly business.

Day 74

We are now sleeping on a wide open verandah which runs around three sides of the upper floor of the hotel, domed openings overlooking the war-damaged streets of Massawa. It is cooler than the room, but the street noises are startlingly close, and late into the night and throughout the early hours trucks rumble by, music echoes from the dozens of coffee shops/cafes/bars which line the narrow streets, children play, their strident voices penetrating the darkness. It is a happy sound and Massawa - in fact all of Eritrea - feels like a safe place; people sleep on narrow home-made beds strung with rope, pressed to the walls of dusty alleys; latticed balconies hang overhead, leaning over the narrow alley ways; men lounge in chairs drinking coffee; and women, seen dimly through doors which open directly onto the street, do their chores by the pale light of home-made lamps. Screaming cats prowl around begging.

But the verandah is cool and quite companionable with other sleepers wrapped like mummies in sheets all about. There is no fear of theft, no suggestion of bodily harm or oppression, just open friendship and interest.

Last night I rammed toilet paper down my ears so deeply to block out the incessant noise that in the morning I couldn't get it out. The more I tried, the deeper I pushed it in. Getting up in the early morning dark and going down the creaking wooden stairs, I broke a twig off a shrub in the courtyard and poked it down my ear to no avail. I began to get claustrophobia. I *had* to get it out. Knowing my efforts were aggravating the problem, I lay and waited until the sun rose and woke Gareth. (That is I woke Gareth; the sun never wakes him.) He tried match sticks and tooth picks, a small key and even the tip of a sharp knife borrowed from the kitchen - nothing would work. I trudged the early morning streets asking in shops for tweezers. Finally, we got a local engineering workshop to sharpen a piece of wire and bend a small hook on the end and, with incredible relief, I managed to hook and winkle the offending lump of paper out.

During the heat of the early afternoon, Gareth and I walked to the end of an unused pier where two ships lay partially submerged and swam with a group of about eight local men. The water was cool and we wished we had goggles. We managed to climb onto the deck of the one partially-submerged ship to jump off into the water, then swam out to the other and explored it. Gareth found some brass name plates that he will try to remove tomorrow, as well as half a human skull, a grim reminder of the recent war.

All hope to visit Libya and Tunisia on our way back home have been abandoned; the air fares to Italy will cripple our budget and time-wise it would be an impossibility. So, sadly, even the token gesture of penetrating the Sahara for 1000km north to south has eluded us. It obviously was not meant to be.

Day 75

Had my hair cut today. A wizened local barber sat me down in his welded barber's chair and on my instructions of "Short, please," proceeded to attack my greying locks with a combination of vigour and a blunt pair of scissors. His technique was primitive but effective. The sides and back got shorter and shorter until I could see my scalp. Then the scissors were laid aside and an antique set of electric clippers turned on; the sides and back became thinner still until I lost my nerve and covered my head with both hands. "The top!" I entreated. "Just the top!" He complied.

I look like an American GI with a beard so I decided to go the whole hog and told him to take the beard off too. The job was rounded off with a liberal dab of evil-smelling methylated spirits and a deft flick of a cow tail fly whisk.

When he saw me, Gareth laughed.

After lunch we swam again in the clear water off the pier and watched local fishermen catch fish with hand lines. It was so clear that we could watch the bait sink deep under the water and see the fish take it. We asked for a go and the smiling youth handed over his line and both Gareth and I pulled in hand-sized fish.

Near evening, quite by chance, we met Greg, the American, and Torban, the Dane (last seen three weeks before in Ethiopia) on their way to the ferry to Jeddah with transit visas to Jordan.

And again the thought: could we have gone that route in the time and with the money available? Saudi, Jordan, Israel, Turkey, Greece, Italy? Perhaps, but the daunting number of visas required and the many ferry crossings make it doubtful and uncertain. Anyway, the die is cast now and our bikes already on their way to Assab and then Italy.

Oh, the tyranny of 'What if's...'!

Had coffee and then a delightful supper with two Namibian girls travelling trans-Africa whom we had met before along the way. We talked and drank red wine until 11 and then bed.

Day 76-77

Another day of waiting, and then another. Walking into town for supper tonight, we decided that tomorrow we will travel the 1,200km desert road to Assab and back by bus/truck and then on to Asmara and Italy. But we met with Angelica and her friend the Namibians and had supper together. David - we met him last at Lalibela - joined us as well as two Germans, two Dutch and an American, all overlanders (they knew all about Gareth and me from the traveller's grape-vine) and during the evening's conversation we realised that we can take the ferry to Jeddah, leaving Friday, then on to Port Suez, see something of

Egypt then on to Alexandria and a ferry to Italy for far less than the air fare alone to Italy.

Immediately we decided to head for Asmara early tomorrow to sort out visas for Saudi Arabia and Egypt. Most exciting to be on the way again!

WEEK 12

Day 78: Tuesday 1 April 1997

Woke early, the sun pale over the still waters of the harbour. A hasty breakfast of 'sunwich' - egg and tomato and onion in an un-buttered bun - and we set off for the bus stop lugging a bag, sleeping bag and crash helmet each. The bus was waiting and we paid our eight Birr and sat down. The Eritrean bus system is good, only seated passengers allowed, each ticket stating seat number, the drivers careful. So un-African, where buses are usually death traps where drivers piloting their un-roadworthy machines vie with each other to see who can break more rules and keep up their average of dead passengers.

Once full, we set off along the coastal plain, a bare desert leading to the massive barrier of purple mountains in the distance. The journey took six hours with two tea stops and a detour where we had to alight and push-start the bus to get it going again. The driver hooted before each hairpin bend all the way up the escarpment because two trucks cannot pass together, needing the whole road to negotiate the turn.

At 1:30pm we were back in Asmara, ate ice cream and doughnuts for lunch and caught a taxi to Dick and Jules. Too late for the Saudi Embassy so made an appointment for 9:00am tomorrow.

Day 79

While having a doughnut and Coke this morning in Asmara waiting for the Saudi Embassy to open, our three German friends walked in looking travel weary. We still don't know their names, it being so convenient always to refer to them as "The Germans", although Gareth calls the one XL - he must be 6ft 7in tall, with long dark-brown hair, a beak nose, perpetually unshaven and sports a small silver ear ring. He hardly ever speaks, his English being weak, but it is probably because he, despite his size, is shy. The three are on their way home now after travelling through Africa for a year and a half.

This casual coming together and separating along the road of fellow travellers has become a special part of our trip as we share mutual acquaintances and always, after the initial questions of "What was X like? And the road? Many punctures? Where are you going from here? Ah, so are we. Travel together?" then come "We saw so and so yesterday; he's heading for...; and the two German girls from Namibia, they're on the ferry with us." And they would say, "Remember Carl the Australian whose bike broke in half? It's welded up now and he's heading south", and we all smile conspiratorially, understanding the implication that the road north was too hard for him.

And what is especially pleasing is that Gareth and I seem to have passed into traveller's lore along the road: "Ah, the father and son on the XT's! We heard about you in Axum and Lalibela!" or, when we meet new travellers, after brief introductions, one might cry, "Oh, yes, the father and son on motorbikes! We've heard about you!" and Gareth and I look at each other and smile, knowing that we must, in some way, be special.

(A disturbing piece of news: Yo Yo - he of the Adventure Overland truck - is 17 days late at his next destination and no one, not even Adventure Overland in London, knows where he is.)

Day 80

With the Saudi visas secured, we were back on the bus to Massawa by 12:30pm. A hot five-hour drive to the coast sitting between two courtly old gentlemen in shammas who shared their roasted peanuts with us and made vague and ineffectual attempts at conversation. Then to the port and customs, bought the ferry tickets and joined Angelica, Andrea and David for supper.

The nights are stifling hot so again I couldn't sleep. A fight in the street below didn't help, with half the occupants of a street bar joining in to separate the two antagonists; and always the noise, music blaring from the doorways of every bar and cafe and the constant passing of trucks. I allowed wisdom to prevail where the toilet paper in the ear trick was concerned and instead got up, slipped on my sandals and spent an hour walking the streets and docks of Massawa at 1am, past noisy bars, marauding cats and alley sleepers snugly wrapped in sheets. In the glare of dock lights, cranes loaded ships and made me think of home.

The ferry leaves tomorrow at 5:00pm. Another day to kill.

Day 81

A cool wind is blowing across dark water and the deep pulse of the ferry engines is felt rather than heard. The sun has set redly against the undulating barrier of purple mountains inland and now they too are disappearing in the salt haze and the fading light. All around us are robed and turbaned Muslims on their way to Mecca; their prayer carpet is just in front of us and a constant stream of bare-foot men prostrate themselves towards the East murmuring with an enviable fervour.

We, the only 'foreigners' - David, Angela, Angelica, Gareth and me - have laid claim to four benches facing each other where our luggage is piled; we intend to lay out our sleeping bags on the benches later and snatch some sleep. Angelica has a fever and has visited the ship's doctor who installed her in a hospital bed, at which we all decided that we too have fevers.

It is good to be heading north again with each beat of the engine. I am sad, though, that I don't have Glyn with me; the ferry has about it an aura of exotic cruises to far-away places which ought to be shared with your wife. And Glyn so loves ship travel.

Day 82-83

The ferry took 42 hours to reach Jeddah with a 4-hour breakdown in mid-ocean. Although the sea was almost continuously flat, I succumbed, as usual, to sea-sickness, particularly when we were becalmed.

The first night, however, I was fine and spent an interesting although uncomfortable night sleeping on the deck just aft of the bow. The stars were clear in an inky sky and a fresh wind blew off the sea. I snuggled down into my sleeping bag but, on the metal deck, I soon realised how bony my body is.

We spent most of the day lying on our benches reading, sleeping and trying to keep the sea-sickness at bay. All about us reclining men hawked and spat with voluptuous enthusiasm while, for hours at a time, the tannoy relayed advice to pilgrims in Arabic about what to expect once they reached Saudi Arabia.

Then, near midday, the first signs of Jeddah appeared over the horizon and by 12:30pm we had docked. I write this at 7:30pm, still sitting in the port offices having papers processed. All about us in this spotless, beautifully built complex are white-robed officials with red tea towels on their heads, soldiers and officials in immaculate khaki, dapper and well-groomed, but painfully under worked. All are men, all sport moustaches. For seven hours (except for an interesting break I'll mention later) we have been moved from one official to another, had our papers checked and rechecked, our bags emptied and searched, felt and probed, and still we are not through. (Gareth's machine gun shells he salvaged from the arms dump in Massawa have gone undetected in his fanny bag, but we felt it wise to dump surreptitiously the piece of human skull we found while swimming from the pier.) Every pilgrim, clutching his meagre belongings in sacks and bags, is thoroughly searched, pushed into lines, moved from one official to another. They submit with stoical resignation.

However, at about 5:00pm, two immaculately groomed gentlemen approached us. They oozed wealth and authority, but not in any unpleasant way. It was impossible not to warm to them. After chatting to us awhile, they insisted that we come with them to see the city of Jeddah so, dressed in our dirty clothes, looking and feeling bedraggled, we climbed into two fancy cars of the large American variety and sped along beautiful palm-lined roads into the centre of Jeddah. The town is immaculate, buildings of glass and marble, exuding wealth. After we had changed money, the two men took us to a traditional restaurant, asked us what we wanted, ordered it and refused any payment.

They then took us on a quick tour of some of the shops in the city centre and what a contrast to Africa! We rubber-necked, conscious of our dirty clothes, at shops selling traditional and Parisian perfumes, R100,000 watches, shops filled with chocolates and nuts and ornate glassware, glazed figs, antiques...

Reluctantly we were pulled away back to the port where, again, we wait.

Italy is still very far away and the ferry is very slow...

It is now 11:00pm and we have missed the ferry.

It is a terrifying thing to have one's life so completely in the hands of faceless officials who speak a foreign language and whose culture is so totally different to one's own. After six hours of being told to go here, sit there, give passports, bring bags, go there, get into line etc etc, we were loaded onto a bus and driven to the ferry. It shone white in the floodlights, the next step closer to home. However, we were met on the ramp by Egyptian officials, our passports demanded and scrutinised. After heated consultation one with another, the captain walked up to us and stated, "No visa, *no go!"*

"But the Egyptian Embassy in Nairobi said that we didn't *need* a visa!" I could hear my voice come dangerously close to begging.

"Who - the consul?"

"No, the lady at the desk - we went to get a visa and she said South Africans don't need visas..."

More officials scrutinised the passports. Telephone calls to the Egyptian police in Cairo. An hour's wait, hanging about on the docks in front of the ramp to the ship. So close! Our traveller friends were all through and settled.

Again the official approached us: "No visa. Sorry. You not go."

And, despite our pleading, Gareth and I, a young man from Eritrea and a middle-aged couple from Sudan with their year-old child, were bundled back into the bus and returned to the waiting room.

Two hours wait.

Lowly officials told us that, if we are not permitted to enter Egypt, we will be shipped back to Massawa...

Suddenly, important looking officials burst into the room. Again we were bundled into a bus. No one told us anything. We managed to discover that it had all been a mistake; we were going. The bus, led by the officials in a car, raced around the harbour, past the ferry which was still at anchor although its gangplank was up, stop here and there, shouted conversation, then back to the waiting room.

No explanation. Another hour's wait.

Then two officials arrived with money and insisted they buy us some food; the money had been provided by the ship's agent, embarrassed at our predicament. There were three ships going to Suez tomorrow, we were assured, and we would be placed on one of them. If not, back to Massawa...

So, we lie on our sleeping bags on the polished floor of the vast and empty arrivals hall, neon lights buzzing, trying to block out the bright white light and hoping that sleep will deaden the feeling of sickness and worry that envelops me. How has our adventure degenerated into this slough of despond?

Day 84

We slept well despite the hard floor and bright lights, the hum of air conditioning all about us; our companions, with whom we have bonded through shared adversity, had curled up on the blue plastic seats and slept, the baby remarkably tolerant, sucking every now and again at her mother's breast.

We are all patient and resigned, knowing that against this faceless efficiency there is no pleading or threatening or bribing. This is the Middle East, not Africa.

There is something strangely and disturbingly intimidating about the Saudi officials, the many badges and dapper uniforms, their clipped beards and moustaches and starched pure-white robes. In the south, with African officials, one has felt free to rant and complain, to attempt to intimidate and even to contemplate bribery. But here, there is a clear compulsion to do what one is told without question, knowing that any attempt to alter one's fate by any method other than a pleasantly phrased request or a throwing of oneself on an official's mercy is doomed to failure if not worse. There is no way I would raise my voice to one of these uniformed men. One has images of dungeons, executions, courts prosecuting with religious fanaticism...

It is a decidedly humiliating experience.

Gareth and I prayed together this morning, desperate prayers, and I prayed with the Sudanese man and his wife and child. They look so pathetic and helpless and lost, he in his rumpled jacket and cheap shoes, an eye which weeps perpetually so that he holds a tissue in one hand to wipe it; she with the uncomplaining acceptance of a peasant woman, the bewildering weight of authority too much for her to understand. They have no money left; yesterday we all clubbed together to make up a $20 shortfall for their ticket to Egypt. Compared to them, we are more than fortunate.

Then at 8:30am the Port Manager arrived, a portly gentleman in pure white robes, immaculate moustache and small goatee as most Saudi men have. He introduced himself as Mr Ahamed and assured us that he would do all he could for us. Half an hour later we were moved to yet another set of blue seats in yet another plastic shining anonymous hall. More waiting. I am reading a book called "The Watch Gods" some garbage set in Egypt with curses and mummies and beautiful women. How they can even publish such stuff, I don't know, but it is the last unread book I have and there is nothing else to do.

At 9:30am Ahamed returned, said that there was no problem and that we would be put on a ferry by 10:30am. He assured us that he had spoken to an Egyptian major who had assured him that there was no problem with our passports.

And so now, we wait until 10:30am (or, as Gareth says, until 12:30pm). He is becoming cynical or perhaps he is just learning the ways of Africa...

WEEK 13

Day 85: Tuesday 8 April 1997

I have just changed my watch back an hour - Egyptian time. For the past 24 hours we have been sailing over oily blue Red Sea waters, the sky clear and pale, the air windless except for the cooling breeze from the ship's motion. There is no movement at all save the gentle vibration of the engine and, in consequence, I have not been sick.

We and our three marooned companions were allowed on the ship with only a cursory glance at our passports and, not quite believing we were finally on board and still expecting a shout from someone with a uniform who had discovered an irregularity, we made our way to the top deck where wooden benches are set out for steerage passengers like ourselves. Others, mainly Arabs, are making themselves comfortable in any sheltered nook of the boat so that often we have to step over bare feet and recumbent forms to move about the ship. In the dining room, through a haze of cigarette smoke, men play dominoes with a grim seriousness and the clack of the pieces can be heard into the night competing with Arab TV.

We have been befriended by an Egyptian deck hand (who claims, repeatedly, to be an English teacher but we struggle to understand a word he says), as well as an Arab group who speak no English and insist we join them playing dominoes. With us, of course, are our Eritrean friend Samuel and the Sudanese family. We all communicate in broken English, smiles, shrugs and hand gestures and I am again conscious of the arrogance of English speakers who naturally assume that all will speak our language while we make little effort to speak theirs. As the saying goes: When a foreigner meets an English speaker, he speaks English. When an English speaker meets a foreigner, he speaks louder.

Everyone is friendly and insists on buying tea, dropping off a cheese sandwich or a cooldrink with a shrug and a shy smile.

Food in the restaurant is limited to rice and a few lumps of overcooked beef, some inedible pickled vegetables, a stale roll and an orange, but it is cheap and filling and Gareth is continually hungry.

Today we have been lying in the sun reading while the wake boils in a straight line to the horizon. We should reach Suez at 7am tomorrow. There is in me a deeply felt knowledge that we are on our way home. As the sun sets red against a still evening sky, pale blue mountains are thrown into relief; we are close to land. The water is oily and smooth and the desert mountains of what has to be Egypt evokes in me a craving for the adventure of travel again. I am frustrated to be covering this distance over water and not astride the motor bikes. The map shows a desert track which runs along the Red Sea coast from Eritrea, through Eastern Sudan and Egypt to the Mediterranean. It is a track which pleads to be explored...

It is now 9:30pm and the darkness has revealed lights on both sides of us, a lighthouse, clusters of smaller lights and the red glow from more distant cities over the horizon. We must be in the narrows where the Red Sea divides to Jordan and Suez.

Tomorrow, Alexandria...

Day 86

It is 8:30pm and we have crossed Africa; granted, not as we had hoped to and not completely on the bikes but it is good to reflect on the fact that outside our hotel window I can hear the bustle and constant blast of hooters which is Alexandria. Both Gareth and I are still firmly of the belief that a true crossing of Africa can only be claimed if one has traversed at least one of the central African countries such as Sudan, Chad, Zaire, Niger, Mauritania and then, of course, Libya or preferably, Algeria - a crossing of the Sahara, in fact, which has unfortunately been denied us.

But back to the ship. At about 11:30pm last night a strong wind came up which buffeted the ship and forced us to curl up inside our sleeping bags to escape from the bitter cold. At 5:30am I couldn't stand the cold or the hard metal deck any longer so I got up and sheltered near the stern, catching the early rays of the sun. The Gulf of Suez had narrowed so that land was clearly visible on both sides, flat desert on the right and a range of desolate rocky mountains which followed the coast on the left.

We entered Suez harbour at 11:00am and waited an interminable two hours (will they turn us away, back to Jeddah, to Massawa? We have come so far, so close... And if we are pushed back, what then?) stomachs knotted with fear before the immigration officers return our passports.

And suddenly we were clear.

No questions, no interrogation, no hitches.

We couldn't believe it. It was too easy. We kept on expecting another check, another official who would find something wrong and call us back. Collect our belongings; a tentative step onto the dock.

No shouts. No one calls us back.

We walk along the docks, past warehouses and offices. Still nothing.

Ahead of us, the harbour gate. Officials checking passports. Knot in the stomach. It has been too easy. They will send us back.

Passports checked. Shake of the head - need to report to customs. Turn back, find the customs offices. Hand over passports again. Stomach knotted. *Stamp stamp*, broad smile. You can go.

Back to the harbour gate. Through!

But again called back - an official wants to see the passports again. Dig them out of the pouch, brief check and a nod.

We are finally through! We are in Egypt! We walk along a road towards the bus station feeling like escaped POW's at large in a foreign land.

How little faith we have.

Suez is a dirty town, filled with paper and overflowing dirt bins and rubble. A cold wind blew grit into our eyes; it seemed that every driver negotiated the roads with one hand on the hooter and men shouted at each other with loud voices. Every man seems to have a cigarette in his mouth. On street corners, old men play dominoes and smoke water-cooled pipes, and cheeky school children walk home.

We waited an hour and a half for the bus to Alexandria (Samuel, our Ethiopian friend, has decided to look after us). The trip itself, which took five hours, was comfortable along good roads which passed through the desert with much military activity and then entered the Nile Delta, with palms and green fields of wheat and rice, but very built up - about 200km of city and suburbs with little or no break between Cairo and Alexandria. Much building of apartment blocks had been taking place on the reclaimed flood plains, a strip of at least 20-25km by 1-2km that we could see, all incomplete apartment blocks, many already occupied and turning rapidly into slum. It seems as if the city or government ran out of money half way through a most ambitious housing project.

We reached Alex at 7:30pm and took a hair raising taxi ride to this cheap hotel. After a hot shower we ventured out to explore our part of the city. It is vibrant and delightful, as different from Addis as Asmara is, and they different from the African cities further south. Where the usual African town and market is an endless repetition of tomato and onion stalls and bloody pieces of hacked meat, Alex is alive with colour and diversity. Hooting cars, clanging yellow trams, street cafes with delicious smells of roasting chicken and liver and onions, potato cakes and schwamas, market stalls selling everything from mounds of fetta cheese and butter, strawberries and oranges, clean stalls of meat with no flies, well cut and displayed, rabbits, pigeons and ducks and chickens alive on display, dates and nuts and pieces of pumpkin and potatoes roasted over coal stoves like miniature steam engines, horse buggies as dapper as an English trap with horses and tack gleaming. A delightful feast for the eyes and nose despite the incessant tooting of horns and suicidal drivers and city dirt and refuse in corners.

Day 87

I started today with a knot in my stomach about the next leg of the trip to Italy, knowing that boats are uncertain and our time rapidly running out; that air tickets will be expensive, perhaps prohibitively so.

We were tramping the streets by 8:00am trying to change money, look for a travel agent/shipping agent/airways office. Everything, of course, was closed and even, after 9:00am, when some businesses had opened, the first five banks wouldn't change travellers cheques and the three shipping companies said: Forget it, you're wasting your time, no ferries run between Egypt and Italy...

Finally we found an airways office open and asked for the cheapest flight to Italy. My budget allowed $520, I felt I could push it to $600 or even, at a pinch, $700 if we live on bread and water, but they quoted $580 *each*.

I felt sick with tension and despair. The thought of tramping Alexandria, coping with a foreign city and a foreign language to try to find a boat depressed me. The boat journey would be at least 4-6 days, if not eight, stopping at Greece and Cyprus, and the bikes are arriving in Italy in five days time, so we will need to be on the boat and sailing almost immediately to be anywhere near on time. And we hadn't even found a shipping company which did the run yet.

Back on the street, we headed in the direction of yet another bank. By chance we passed a Lufthansa office and called in.

"Your cheapest flight to Italy!" I begged. "Special discount, student fare, no frills, etc etc."

A most efficient young man, fluent in English, tapped at his computer while I held my breath. He looked up. "For your son," he said, "$265 and for you $480."

I could have kissed him! We were home!

We changed enough money to cover the fare and living expenses and returned only to be told that he'd made a mistake. Italy doesn't allow South Africans into the country on a one-way ticket. We would have to buy return tickets and there was no student discount on the round trip.

My heart dropped and I felt numb with despair. After having come SO close...

I asked him to repeat the fare, did a quick mental calculation and realised we could do it - at a pinch. $840 for both tickets. More than the $700 tops, but significantly less than the $1160 quoted by the other agency.

I booked and paid. A flood of relief passed over me; I felt light with joy and an uncontrollable urge to laugh came over me! We fly via Malta, leaving Cairo at 2:30am the day after tomorrow so we will just be able to squeeze in a look at the pyramids.

I was able to contemplate the rest of the day with a sense of carefree abandon. Only one real hurdle left: will the bikes arrive safely and on time?

We spent the rest of the day walking about the streets of Alexandria (or at least a tiny part of it) covering about 30km during the day. We explored endless little dark alleys with ancient overhanging buildings and balconies, sniffing in dusty shops (especially, for Gareth, those selling or repairing antique clocks!). We followed the road along the bay with rocking fishing boats and a 13th century fort built on the site of the original Alexandria lighthouse; we sampled delicious local foods from dingy restaurants down side streets and on pavements, taking our lives in our hands crossing roads, petting the hundreds of street cats, talking to the horses and generally pigging out on the exotic fascination of a city I could spend a month in. Its size is awesome, disappearing along the curve of the coast as far as the eye can see, a turbulent bustle of a city, ancient and varied and fascinating. And my lightness of spirit enabled me to enjoy it even more!

It was strange to think of my father here 50-odd years ago as a young man during the war, walking these same streets, being hit by a car (that's not hard to believe!) and spending months, fly-pestered, in a hospital. As we walked, I tried to imagine him here, take myself back to that time, see it through his eyes. It made him feel close, this man who is my father and who brought me up, walked and cycled with me to Lourenco Marques and Beira, helped to make me who I am, and it was good to be able to tell Gareth about him.

Tomorrow Cairo and then Malta, Rome, home!

Day 88

Bus to Cairo, the trip spoilt by the incessant smoking of the Egyptian men and the screening of an inane video throughout the trip. It is sad that modern man seems incapable of sitting quietly for a few hours with his thoughts or watching the passing scenery. I sometimes long for quietness and solitude as a balm for frayed nerves.

We spent a frustrating two hours in Cairo looking for a cheap room for Samuel (who is still with us) then left our bags and did the pyramids! Obviously our appreciation of them was limited by a lack of time and money and, for me, by the knowledge that Glyn so badly wants to see them that our visit almost smacks of betrayal. But it would have been silly to deny ourselves the experience on those grounds and I know Glyn wouldn't have expected it.

Afterwards we killed a few hours walking about the city, abustle with life, ate a cheap supper and, at 9:30pm (unable to wait any longer despite being five hours early) said our goodbyes to Samuel and took a taxi to the airport. The taxi driver, in usual taxi-driver spirit, tried to get ten pounds off me for parking instead of the required one, but (from long experience of people trying to remove money from my pocket into their own) I asked the price of parking from a policeman. Gareth is embarrassed by my outraged arguments with people who attempt to rip me off, but it angers me so much. "Why are you trying to cheat me?" I demand. "Why did you say ten pounds when it is one? Why are you trying to cheat me?"

After a four-hour wait we took off at 2:30am, leaving African soil with a sense of sadness tinged with excitement at the thought of going home. Three hours to Malta, a four-hour wait in the transit lounge where the plot of a novel which has been knocking at the door for a year or so popped into my head. I retired into the lavatory and furiously jotted down notes on the back of a letter I had in my pouch. I think my mind already has accepted the end of the trip and is starting to look ahead to normality again which, I hope, means some productive writing. Then, at 9:30am, we took off for Rome.

Day 89

I write this sitting in the waiting room of Rome central station feeling scratchy-eyed, drugged with physical and emotional exhaustion, lonely and homesick. Large cities always have this effect on me; they produce a frightening loneliness and isolation amongst their crowded streets, an impersonal sidelining of everything that is personal and human and vulnerable.

We arrived from the warmth and blue Red Sea skies of Africa to a dull rainy European day. The sense of foreignness and isolation was greater, is greater, than I have felt at any time in Africa, except perhaps trapped within the bureaucracy of Jeddah. Very few people speak or understand English and some, when approached, ignore me with disdain. It makes me feel like a tramp, a beggar, it demeans my person. I realise, however, in mitigation, that, unshaven, unwashed and rather smelly, we probably look like tramps.

Gareth and I have realised with a shock that existing in Europe is somewhat different to the cheaper and more relaxed Africa. Our total daily budget of $35 (which supported us throughout Africa, paying for food, accommodation, transport, repairs and sundries), upped to $39 for Europe (it's all we have), is laughably inadequate. The cost of the cheapest hotel room in Rome is double our entire daily budget and then some; no food, no transport, no petrol.

Eventually we were directed to a place close to the station that offers a place to sleep cheaply. Again the realisation that we look rather down on our luck was reinforced because the place turned out to be a shelter for the homeless. Unfortunately it was for women only so, with the rain pouring down outside, we were given directions to the men's hostel via a no. 714 bus, but it only opens after 8:00pm.

We sat disconsolately on a sheltered step on the side of the road, waiting for the rain to ease, and realised that, financially, we are simply not going to make it. The only solution is to head back faster, cutting out days. This, with a sense of relief, we have decided to do. Arrival of the bikes permitting, we will try to get back a week early.

The rain having eased, we made a dash for the central railway station, hunted unsuccessfully for a place to wash, got information about the cost and times of trains to Livorno (no buses take that route) and sat out the afternoon in this waiting room. Life has hit rock bottom and now it is time to go home; however, tomorrow is Sunday and a French visa is still lacking so, sadly, we must wait. Again...

At 6:00pm we found the 714 bus and asked the driver whether he could drop us off near the shelter but he couldn't understand us and didn't know where the address was. But again God was good. A small man with a limp, obviously destitute, saw the pamphlet I had been given and it turned out that he was going there and, without understanding a word he said, he assured us that he would take us there. This was most fortunate because we would never have found the place, let alone known where to get off the bus, which wound its way into and through a maze of streets, and after 20 minutes we alighted. The small man chatted to us amicably in Italian all the time; we smiled and shrugged in reply.

I picked up a 1000 lira note on the road which I gave to our new friend who promptly called in at the nearest bar and drank it, explaining the source of his garrulousness!

Then from 6:30pm to 8:30pm we sat on a cold wall outside a deserted building. Darkness fell and cold crept into our bones. The destitute, tramps as well as quite respectable looking men and women of all ages, gathered until about 35 of us were hanging around hugging ourselves to keep away the cold. Most smoked; an old man coughed tubercularly, hawking and spitting on the path. Some were obviously drunk. A woman with tight tiger-skin pants and bulging carry bags joked with the men. All spoke Italian; all ignored us.

Finally at 8:30pm a light came on. A man appeared at the top of a flight of stairs, clip board and pen in his hands. He began to call out names. People clustered forward hopefully, like Mary and Joseph afraid of being told there was no more room. We remained in the background, ignored, ashamed and out of place.

Mixed feelings were racing through my mind, and Gareth's too, as I found out later. We both felt very much like beggars and, in a way, we were. We hadn't slept more than an hour the night before, we were dirty and exhausted and, in all truthfulness, simply didn't have the money to hire a room for the next few nights and hope to make it home on the money that was left. But deep inside we both felt like frauds, knowing that we do have money, far more than the others around us. Also, there is more than enough money in our bank account in Wales and it would only take a visit to the bank to access it. But, on principle, I want to complete the trip on the money we have, don't want to phone Glynis and ask her to bail us out, pay more of our dwindling finances to what I'm sure she feels is a glorified holiday.

Finally there were five of us left. The man with the clipboard waved three young men angrily away and then turned to us and gestured for us to come closer. I felt strangely close to tears, wanting so badly to be invited in, needing the warmth and security, the comfort of a friendly face.

"Your son?" he asked and I nodded. "Come -"

As we walked in, he shouted at the three youths again to go. Thinking we had taken the last beds available and denied those more deserving of shelter, I asked the man to allow them in; we would sleep on the floor, I said, indicating our sleeping bags.

But it seems there is a system in place here to prevent the destitute making the shelter a permanent home: two weeks and then they must leave and fend for themselves for at least a month before being allowed back for a further two weeks.

Our night in the shelter for homeless persons was a moving one for me and, I know, for Gareth. We have been welcomed, given a mat and a blanket and shown into a room with five others. A space on the floor has been made for us; we unroll our sleeping bags and sit down. A sense of grateful relief has come over me. The man in charge shows us the bathroom and tells us that if we want soap or a razor, shampoo or shaving cream we will be given these from the store. We can wash clothes if we want and they will give us washing soap. The bathroom is spotless.

After a glorious shower and with newly washed underpants, shirt and socks over the heater to dry, we are told to get in line for coffee and a roll. We accept the cold coffee gratefully but refuse the roll because we have eaten but more, I think, because of a sense of guilt at our seeming hypocrisy. Gareth, I am pleased to note, refused his too. He has a more highly developed sense of what is morally right than I have, most times, which gives me a great sense of pride in him.

And then, sleep numbing my mind and pressing on my eyelids, we climb into our sleeping bags, clean and warm and wanted. Next to us, on the floor, a young man kneels to pray. His wife lies next to him. After his prayers he lies down but rouses himself after a moment and nudges me. Speaking in signs, he asks me whether I will move my shoes to the other side of the room because they smell...

Day 90

After a good night's sleep we were woken with loud shouts at 6:30am. The complex was abustle with people dressing, folding up blankets and mats, queuing at the bathroom and lining up for coffee. Regulations stipulated that we had to be out by 7:00am. Nothing could be left in the building so Gareth and I were again saddled with our bags, helmets and sleeping bags.

We caught the bus to the central terminal, managed to leave the bags at a left luggage, bought a map of Europe in readiness for the trip home and, armed with our tourist guide to Rome, headed on foot for the Tiber. The day was cold but clear and in no time we were at the Colosseum, marvelling at the relics of the Roman Empire (and, of course, the cats). With the whole day at our disposal, we walked all over, getting lost down small cobbled streets and taking in the sights.

At last we came to St.Peters and, expecting to be turned away by a prohibitively high entrance fee, were pleasantly surprised to be allowed in free. And, oh! what a moving experience. I stood before the Pieta with tears in my eyes at the sheer beauty of it, the mixture of love and sadness in Mary's face, an acceptance of Jesus' death, a pride in what he had done and yet the deep anguish that his death caused her. What genius to express such emotions in stone. One could almost see the cloth of her gown move to the softness of her breathing. The church is vast and perfect in its construction, so beautiful and so obviously built to the glory of God that one is left with the dual sense of one's own insignificance and God's greatness. In that building there is no place for pettiness, and the glory of God's perfection is so palpable that one feels uplifted in one's soul. I sat quietly for a while in a side chapel and prayed, wanting so deeply to be more worthy of God and the world and my wife and family.

This evening, waiting in the cold and dark to be let into the shelter again, John, an Englishman who had grown tired of the predictability of English life, and Carlo, an Italian who spoke fluent English and who worked for a priest ("For the *priest*, not the church," he insisted), gave us the run down on how to avoid being caught by bus inspectors while riding the buses without a ticket; how and where to get free meals - a different charity for each meal on each day of the week; where some charities give out small envelopes of money to the destitute; where to get blankets and old clothes and even free cigarettes; where in the station to sleep and how to prevent being mugged. There is an information chain for the tramps and destitutes (or for those who choose to be destitute) in the same way one functions for travellers; instead of: X is a cheap hotel and at Y they serve cheap fish on Tuesdays, here it is free breakfast at this church between 8:30am and 9:00am on Wednesdays and on Friday evenings that shelter offers a three-course meal with five cigarettes.

We accepted the coffee and bun tonight, then lay on our mats. A young man next to me informed me in broken English that he was just one day out of a two-year drug rehabilitation programme and his father won't have him back home until he has proved himself first. He needs a job.

Day 91

A traumatic day. We walked to St.Peters after taking a bus to the centre of Rome (watching out, as instructed, for the inspectors, knowing now what they look like, and ready to jump from the bus and run!), left our bags (for free as instructed) at the church and found the French embassy. After a half hour wait during which we filled in forms (more complicated than any we'd filled in before - this is Europe, not Africa) we were ushered in. A rather brusque woman listened briefly to our story then informed us with a curl to her lip that visas simply couldn't be issued. Her tone implied that we had rather a cheek even presuming such a thing. We had: NO return ticket (I explained the purpose of our journey), NO travel insurance (ours was valid for Africa only), NO documents for the bikes (they were aboard the Omo Wonz somewhere at sea) and NO proof of sufficient funds (I feared she would ask me to produce the thin wad of a mixture of lira, French franks and dollars I had left).

The woman left us while she discussed the matter with the consul. I waited, numb with fear and depression and mumbling an incantation of meaningless prayer. After an interminable wait, she returned to inform us that at the very least we would require: insurance, papers for the bikes and proof of adequate funds. "Get the papers from the motorbikes and you can go to the embassy in Milan. Goodbye."

I feel quite sick with depression. The barriers against us getting through and home seemed to be mounting, not falling away.

We collected our bags and rushed back through the centre of Rome to the train station, just in time to catch the 12.35pm to Livorno. It was an unpleasant three-hour journey because of the tension in my stomach regarding our future. Furthermore, we had eaten nothing since the roll and coffee the night before. I wasn't particularly hungry, but Gareth must have been ravenous but, as usual, he didn't complain.

We arrived in Livorno at 3:40pm, had a quick bite to eat at the station cafe, then caught two buses to the Piazza Attias and, rushing to get there before closing time, found the offices of the shipping agent. Fortunately the manager, a delightful man called Antonio Pacelli, spoke fluent English but he had further devastating news: "I'm sorry," he informed us, "the Omo Wonz has been delayed two weeks in Assab with engine trouble. It has only left for Italy this morning. We expect it to arrive in 11-12 days..."

I was close to tears of despair and frustration. My stomach knotted again as my mind raced, looking for alternatives, ways out of the maze we were trapped in like rats. A 12-day wait in a strange town, facing European costs with almost no money. The thought of being home in ten days which had warmed me over the previous days and weeks now stretched to three weeks and still the uncertainty of the French visa. And will the Italian visa still be valid after all that time?

All at the office gathered to offer assistance. Secretaries phoned around, looking for cheap accommodation: there was none because of the influx of Afghanistan refugees. Antonio and his partner Elio debated possibilities in Italian and made more calls. I imagined us finding a sheltered doorway somewhere and curling up in our sleeping bags.

I asked if I could fax Glyn and they insisted that I phone. Jem answered and, instead of talking to her (Gareth and I had been incommunicado for the past two weeks) I asked flatly, "Is Mom there?" My voice was so filled with despair and held-back tears that she thought her brother had been killed and I was phoning to relay the bad news. But what a pleasure to hear Glyn's voice, solid and comforting and needing me back. She understood and would look into the medical insurance. She accepted the delayed return date with reasonable pragmatism.

So, what were our options? Wait the 12 days or fly to Wales and then back when the bikes arrive or take a train to Wales or fly and freight forward the bikes to the UK. The last seemed the most logical under the circumstances although an anti-climactic end to our trip. But soon that idea was scotched because the freight alone would be at least $1000. Then Elio phoned the local travel agent and established that a charter flight to Gatwick leaves three times a week from Pisa, the price within our budget. Finally they managed to contact an ex-South African woman, Maria, just five minutes walk from the offices, who has agreed to put us up for the night.

So here we are, clean and showered, in a lovely room with the prospect of flying home on Thursday; sadly the first plane available. If we do this, we can sort out the French visa (and another Italian visa) from London and fly back on the 26th and then ride home.

So, light at the end of a very dark tunnel.

Home - Part 1

Day 92

Slept the sleep of the emotionally exhausted to wake at 9:30am. Gareth, of course, still asleep. I wonder if he would ever wake up if I didn't prod him to consciousness each day.

We have made the decision to fly home on Thursday and booked the flight and return on Thurs 8th April. By then the bikes will be here and cleared and we will complete the journey in the saddle - an emotionally satisfying conclusion, I think, and one very necessary after the traumas and disappointments of the last six weeks. Not twenty minutes after I had made the booking, a fax from Glyn arrived suggesting exactly the same thing; in fact urging it because she and Jemma "really need to be a family again".

So, what a joy it was to phone her and tell her we will be home in two days and not 21. I reflect too on my feelings and thoughts early in the trip about our relationship and whether, after three months, Glynis might have decided that life without me was, in fact, quite hassle free and not really want me back. My deep desire is to be reunited with her and my daughter, and her desire to have me back is of great significance at our age, a time when so many marriages are becoming stale and dead and so many men, especially, start to look elsewhere to replace that which has gone. These three months have been good for me to reflect on my life, what is important and what not, my relationship with Glyn away from the day-to-day grind which so often clouds the real issues.

And so, in light and carefree frame of mind, Gareth and I bought wrapping paper and tape, dragged out all the gifts we have accumulated over the three months and thirteen countries, and wrapped them. What fun we had!

Day 94

I write this in the MacDonalds at Gatwick Airport as Gareth and I wait, yet again; two hours this time for the next bus to Newport. It seems that fate or whatever has decided to have a final go at us.

After Antonio dropped us off at Pisa Airport we waited two and a half hours before boarding the Air Caledonia flight; and I must admit to a lump in my throat when I heard the lovely Scottish accent of the flight attendant welcoming us aboard. We were finally on our way home!

The flight to Gatwick was uneventful; England was cloudy and chilly when we landed but, instead of walking hassle-free into the country of our adoption, we were faced with yet another barrier. It was only when we joined the queue at Immigration that I gave our admittance into the United Kingdom a moment's thought. That, surely, was the least of our problems. I mean, we'd just travelled across Africa. We reached the front of the queue. A pleasant official asked, "And how long will you be staying in the UK?"

Not expecting this question, I hesitated and then said, cheerfully, "As long as possible!"

She paused with a little frown on her face. "There might be a small problem," she said, seeing that we had no visas in our passports.

Silent prayers again and the old familiar knot in my stomach. Why I have not bled to a slow and horrible death by now from multiple ulcers I don't know.

What followed was the final, I hope, twist of the knife: nearly two hours of question and answer, copious taking of notes and the serving on us of a document whose ominous opening statement assured us that: "YOU ARE A PERSON LIABLE TO BE DETAINED"!

We are required to report to Gatwick on 11 April for an interview with the immigration authorities who will decide on our fate. I may not work; if Gareth and I leave the country i.e. to go to Italy to fetch the bikes, we stand a very good chance of not being allowed back in, turned away at the border and sent back to South Africa.

Sadly, the interview caused us to miss the bus to Wales by five minutes; next bus 7:05pm - a two-hour wait. Phoned Glyn and told her to expect us at 10:35pm which sadly has spoiled the welcome home party she had organised.

The struggle to get home has truly become a nightmare.

And so, once again, we wait the two hours for the bus...

A Week Later

And now, a week later, I sit in the dining room of our house typing these notes, trying to decipher my scrawl written in various dingy rooms, in the heat and surrounded by the flies of Africa. Again, I wait - this time three weeks for the interview with British Immigration.

What do I feel?

Unsure of myself. Africa is very far away, its smells and sounds, the people we met, the things we saw. The bikes are still somewhere on the Red Sea, but we are prevented from fetching them. In a way, I am a guest in my own home, Glynis and Jemma having developed a routine in which Gareth and I played no part. And in a way, I am a guest in this country too, having been given temporary admission only. I am not permitted to work, pending the enquiry into my status, so I hang about, filling time.

So, I have whiled away my days typing this diary, thinking about the future.

Have we done the right thing? What will the future hold...

Home - Part 2

Thursday 19 June.

Letters instructing Gareth and me to report for deportation back to South Africa had been typed and signed. Fortunately, though, despite this, we managed to convince the authorities to allow us to stay in the UK. The details are unimportant; this amazing country is now our home. We have the documents that say so.

The day that permission to stay in the UK arrived, Gareth and I boarded a bus for London to get our French and Italian visas and purchase one-way tickets to Italy. The final leg of our journey has begun.

Not having been able to work since we arrived here, funds are frighteningly low. After landing in Pisa late in the evening, Gareth and I found a secluded spot on the disused upper floor of a parking garage in Pisa Airport to lay out our sleeping bags. Throughout the night the wind buffets outside and swirls around us on the hard concrete. To one side the motorway roars.

The next day we take a train and bus to Livorno and into the warm embrace of Antonio Pacelli and his colleagues who lead us through the nightmare maze of Italian bureaucracy, from office to office and official to official, a five-hour process which takes us, at last, to a massive dusty shed in a corner of the docks. Another wait until the right key is procured. We can see a thin strip of the bikes through a gap between the doors. They look forlorn and I wonder whether they will even start and how much damage to them has been done.

At last the door swings open. The bikes are covered in dust; rust has stained all unpainted surfaces; one tyre is flat and the locks on our bags have been ripped open. This is to be expected, but annoying just the same. We wheel them out and quickly check the load: socket set and my gloves stolen but, fortunately, nothing else. Gareth pumps his tyre and, after a top-up of petrol and a few kicks, both engines fire. A sense of elation comes over me; what a glorious sound!

We say our goodbyes and ride through the streets of Livorno and onto the motorway.

Having been warned that in Italy, one has to be over 21 to ride a motorcycle over 350cc, I am horrified to be waved to the side of the road by two policemen wearing black leather and dark glasses. They aren't smiling.

"Drivers' licences," they demand.

I dig in my pouch and pass over the two international drivers' licences, mine legal, Gareth's forged and him still two days short of his eighteenth birthday. Please, Lord, we have come so far... I plead silently. From where I stand I can see the Tippex where I altered Gareth's ID number from my 51 to his 79, the years of our birth. It is impossible that this terrifying figure of authority hidden behind the anonymity of his black leather jacket and dark glasses will not see it too. What do they do in Italy to people who forge a driver's licence and then ride un-roadworthy motor cycles under age? - (my back tyre is almost smooth, Gareth's lights don't work and my indicator switch mechanism has been damaged on the ship).

After a long and tense silence the illegal documents are handed back. They don't check the bikes, instead wave us on with a contemptuous flick of the finger. They do not smile. Quickly we kick the engines alive and ride on, fearful of being called back for further scrutiny.

And so, across northern Italy, over high mountains and through a hundred tunnels. Gareth, without lights, finds the tunnels a nerve-wracking business and, after a detour to look at the leaning tower and a night in a camp site just outside Genoa, the rain comes. We ride hour after hour in the freezing cold, a bully of a wind hitting at us, our dirty yellow rain suits doing a pretty good job of keeping us dry. Saturday night finds us caught by darkness and rain. Off the side of the road we see an abandoned farmer's shed and make for it. Long grass shelters the bikes from view of the road. The shed is a rickety affair, just a tiled roof held up by rotting poles. It has been built to shelter four old flat-bed wagons, covered in a fur of dust - but it seems almost homely compared to the rain outside.

We unload and lay out our sleeping bags on a patch of wagon bed that seems dry but, as the rain strengthens, drips begin to fall on us with frustrating regularity. We move again and again, finally settling for the least drippy spots and accepting that a completely dry night is going to elude us. As the light fades and inside the shed becomes deep shadow, we lie on our sleeping bags and listen to the drip of the rain and the mournful complaining of birds. Home is still a long way away, the future still uncertain.

Tomorrow Gareth turns eighteen, becomes a man. And I reflect again on how proud I am of him, my tall gangling son. Throughout the long cold ride, the damp sleeping bags, the annoying drips from a leaking roof he has not complained. There has never been a complaint, not in four months, hardly ever in eighteen years. His quaint and endearing stoicism still holds firm. I love and respect him greatly.

Morning wakes us with the steady drip of rain. We pack damp bedding, pull on damp clothes and load sodden bikes.

And then over the Alps, snow-covered and misty, and into France. We travel steadily and make good time. Rain and wind still pummel us, but the countryside is beautiful, the roads good and well sign-posted and the small towns through which we pass delightfully quaint. More and more motorcyclists, singly but most often in groups, flash past us, leather-clad, their machines gleaming and high-tec. We plod along, our bikes dirty, damaged, rusty, engines clattering. I feel like the old train that needed to get over the hill - *Gotta make it, gotta make it, gotta make it. You'll never make it, you're too small...*

Many of the bikers wave as they pass. Now I don't know whether they wave at every gleaming machine they pass, or whether they are singling us out - recognising something that we personify, tatty and road-weary that we are.

I like to think it's that.

Our torn jeans and cheap plastic rain jackets are an embarrassment compared with their expensive leathers; our bikes an anachronism, typewriters in the age of computers. But we have achieved something, a middle-aged man and a boy. Our clothes, machines and our bodies bear scars from these past 15,000 kilometres and four months; our minds are full of memories. And I think the wave from passing bikers is an acknowledgement of that. And I cannot but help think of the young men in Pretoria, just days into our trip, who called out of the windows of their cars at us:

Where you from?

Ixopo -

Good luck!

We were wearing our yellows then too, bright and embarrassingly clean. I remember feeling a fraud and longing for the time I could say with honesty that we had earned their looks of envy and respect.

I think we have earned it now and tomorrow we will be home...

POSTSCRIPT

It's now 2017 and I've just gone through my diary. Reading it again after all these years has been a rewarding and somewhat emotional experience. If you've got this far, I will assume you might be interested in how things turned out for the Bransby family. After all, I have sub-titled this book "A Father's Diary" and so:

Glynis and I recently celebrated our 43rd wedding anniversary. She still hates motor bikes but is tolerant of my desire to head off each year into the unknown on my bike.

My daughter, Jemma, (who, although she doesn't have much part in this tale, is just as precious and loved as her elder brother) qualified as a chiropractor, married a chiropractor and have given us two grandchildren who dominate me with ruthless efficiency.

Me? I managed, after five long and frustrating years, to get back into my chosen profession of teaching; the last ten years teaching bright-eyed and receptive primary school children I regard as one of the most special times of my life. I retired in 2013.

And Gareth? He is now a successful qualified engineer - software, electronic, marine, whatever. A young man of high intelligence and eclectic interests.

And does he still enjoy riding bikes? I hear you ask. Or is he like the young man in "Smith and Son" I mentioned earlier who was dragged off by his father, eager to recapture a precious moment in his life, on an ill-conceived and ultimately frustrating motorcycle journey? I am pleased to say: yes, he still rides bikes and no, he's not like Mr Smith's son. Not only that, but over the last few years he and I have embarked on some amazing motorcycle adventures together, first to Russia, then to Morocco and, over the past three years, into Central Asia. I have written travelogues of all five trips, if you are interested: "Venture into Russia: Three Motorcycle Journeys"; "There are no Fat People in Morocco", "The Wakhan Corridor: A Motorcycle Journey into Central Asia" and "A Pass too Far".

I had to smile, though, when I read in my trans-Africa diary that, at the age of 45, I regarded our trip as a "once-in-a-lifetime" event and felt that, even then, I was getting beyond it. And now, in my sixties, I am still enjoying riding my bike and sharing that joy with my son. I expect that we will continue to ride together for many more years...

Other books by Lawrence Bransby:

Travelogues:

A Pass too Far
Travels in Central Asia

Trans-Africa by Motorcycle
A Father's Diary

By Motorcycle through Vietnam
Reflections on a Gracious People

There are no Fat People in Morocco

Venture into Russia
Three Motorcycle Journeys

The Wakhan Corridor

A Walk to Lourenco Marques
Reminiscences of a 13-year-old

By Bicycle to Beira
Reminiscences of a 15-year-old

Adult Novels:

Life-Blood - Earth-Blood

A Matter of Conscience

Second Sailor, Other Son

Novels for Young Adults:

Down Street
Winner of the MER Prize for Youth Literature

Remember the Whales
Winner of the J.P. van Der Walt Prize

A Mountaintop Experience
Book Chat South African Book of the Year 1993

The Geek in Shining Armour

Of Roosters, Dogs and Cardboard Boxes

The Boy who Counted to a Million
Winner of the Sir Percy Fitzpatrick Prize;
MNET Award Finalist '96

Outside the Walls

Manufactured by Amazon.ca
Acheson, AB

13688167R00132